PROFESSIONAL CENTRE

Teaching in the smaller school

Holywell Primary School, Tawstock, North Devon

Teaching
in the smaller school

Bill Forward

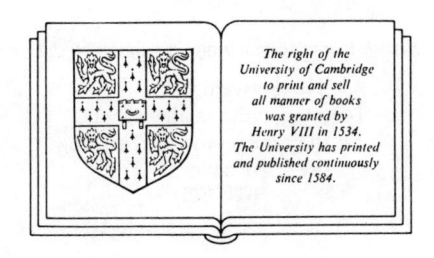

CAMBRIDGE UNIVERSITY PRESS
Cambridge
New York   New Rochelle
Melbourne   Sydney

Published by the Press Syndicate of the University of Cambridge
The Pitt Building, Trumpington Street, Cambridge CB2 1RP
32 East 57th Street, New York, NY 10022, USA
10 Stamford Road, Oakleigh, Melbourne 3166, Australia

© Cambridge University Press 1988

First published 1988

Printed in Great Britain at the University Press, Cambridge

British Library cataloguing in publication data:
Forward, Bill
Teaching in the smaller school.
1. Small Primary schools. Teaching
I. Title
372.11'02

ISBN 0 521 34816 1

Contents

	Acknowledgements	viii
	Preface	ix
	Introduction	xi
1	**Organising space**	**1**
	Junior room	3
	Infants room	5
	Teaching together	7
	The two-teacher school – The three-teacher school	
	Laying out the units	14
	Practical considerations	
	A final comment	15
2	**Teaching mixed age and ability classes**	**17**
	Grouping the children	19
	Larger than class-sized groups – Class-sized groups – Smaller groups	
	Individualised learning	22
	Avoiding repetition	24
	The small school and the under-5s	25
	Opportunities in the mixed age/ability class	26
	Summary	
	Organising time: responses to the mixed age/ability class	28
	Simulated classroom models	28
	Junior room – Teaching together: a two-teacher primary school – Teaching together: a two-teacher junior co-operative unit in a three-teacher primary school	
	Examples of current practice	39

vi   *Contents*

          Primary school with junior co-operative unit – Primary school with infants co-operative unit – Primary school: the infants room

          A final comment   53

3   Curriculum opportunities   **55**

    Curricular aims   56
        A persuasive society – Technology – A threatened environment

    Knowledge, skills and personal qualities   59
        Being knowledgeable in relevant ways – Locating and validating knowledge – Using knowledge – Thinking critically – Personal qualities – Summary

    An opportunity for the small school   62

    Using the environment   62

    Simulated classroom models   65
        Warner's Wood

    Using the community   69

    Simulated classroom models   70
        Stillwood, a village study – 'Neighbours', an inner-city study

    Project approach   81
        Preparation – Organisation – The project plan – Session pattern – The display – Content – Social and personal development – Aesthetic development – Co-operation

    Examples of current practice   87
        A primary school

    A final comment   90

4   The headteacher's role   **92**

    The head as leader   93

    The head as administrator   96

    The head and curriculum policy   99

    The head and staff   101

    The head as evaluator   101

    The head and other schools   103

    The head and the community   104

    Examples of current practice   104

    A final comment   107

5	**Staff support and professional development**	**109**
	(a) Classroom support	109
	Support from the headteacher – Other support	
	(b) Professional development	112
	(c) Career aspirations	115
	At national level – At local authority level – At school level	
	(d) Support for headteachers	119
	The headteacher's aide	
	A final comment	121
6	**The school and the community**	**123**
	The community supports and uses the school	124
	Parents in school – Adults, experts and otherwise, in school – Societies and associations in school	
	The school supports and uses the community	130
	The very young – The elderly – The disadvantaged – Community activity	
	Examples of current practice	135
	An urban primary school	
	A final comment	140
7	**The local education authority and the small school**	**141**
	Responsibilities	141
	Patterns of support	142
	Staffing – Resources – Overcoming isolation	
	Co-operative groups of small schools (COSS groups)	148
	Setting up small COSS groups – Co-operative activities within a small COSS group	
	Larger co-operative groups	153
	Examples of current practice	154
	LEA no. 1 – LEA no. 2 – LEA no. 3	
	Summary	159
	A final comment	159
	Postscript	161
	Further reading	165

Acknowledgements

Particular thanks to the teachers and children who allowed me to visit their schools and draw on their experience:

    Stonesfield Primary School
    Green Mount Primary School
    Kentisbury Primary School
    Woolhampton Primary School
    Bishop's Nympton Primary School
    Middle Barton Primary School
    Pilton Infants School

I am indebted to the following headteachers and teachers who dealt so patiently with yet another interruption and gave so generously of their time: Pam Cruse, Al Cruse, Anne Parnell, Andy Rowe, Garry Reed, Adrian White, June Mitchel, Judith Sing, Chris Jolly, Hugh Protherough, Martin Norton, Connie Brownjohn, Jennifer Aker and Mrs F. P. Kunz.

My thanks also to the following LEA advisers and inspectors who so kindly supplied me with so much information on the activities of their own authorities relating to small schools: John Litson, Kay Jones, Peter Busby, Jack Tempest, Sheila Addison and Rodney King.

Bill Forward

Preface

Mariansleigh and Romansleigh Parochial – an impossibly beautiful name to apply to any small school – lies remote and hidden in the North Devon countryside. It was my first encounter with such a place. Lately home from sea, but accepted for training college, I was considered, in 1947, ready to teach by an authority desperate to stand anyone in front of a class. Access to the two-teacher school was by the tree-tunnelled lanes of pre-hedge-flail Devon. It was a leaf-bound, grass-dreaming place not remotely connected to the wartime western ocean and the distant seas I had just left. I fell in love with it and have been in love with small schools ever since.

I spent the summer term that year playing lunchtime cricket with the children and warding off the occasional marauding county inspector while the headmistress took the remnants of the lunch home to her cottage and her pigs – no one wasted food in a nation that was still strictly rationed. The children, unsophisticated but full of the common sense of the countryside, kept me softened up with wild strawberries and flowers picked from the hedgerows. They piled into the back of my open car at 4 o'clock and I dropped them off at their cottages and hamlets on my way back to town.

The images of that summer have never left me, and led after college and a short spell of secondary teaching, back to small primary schools and eventual headship of one on the Dartmoor fringe, even more remote than Romansleigh. Later, after urban headships, came a period as one of the county advisers, who in Devon had replaced local inspectors in the supervision of schools. For a number of years I edged my way up those same green tunnels to emerge into quiet village squares and streets searching for one of the 200 small schools that Devon supports. Without fail the sorcery that had been woven at Romansleigh returned with the first step through the school door. The classroom now is a little more colourful perhaps, the short trousers of the boys and the cotton dresses of the girls replaced by jeans and sweatshirts, the teachers seemingly younger and more full of ideas – but there is the same strong sense of each child knowing and being known, of belonging.

Small schools then to me, and to many others, are special places, essential to keep as part of the educational provision for our children. But not all those in authority are enchanted by small schools. They are expensive to run and seem often to lack the facilities that larger establishments offer. In a real world which emphasises the advantages of merger and the efficiency of scale, small schools have to prove themselves again and again as effective educational units. Enchanting as the 'wild strawberry' song may be, there is more demanding music to dance to now and we do no favour to our small school if we don't recognise this.

This book is not another hymn of praise to the small school. It starts from the premise that those who teach in them are aware of the advantages that flow from knowing children well over an extended period, and of the sort of unique, supportive relationships which can grow between child and teacher in that time. They don't need to be told that small numbers allow for a more total involvement of all the children or of the confidence, self-reliance and responsible attitudes that can develop in pupils who mix all day with older and younger children. They don't need to be told how much fun it can all be. If they have any qualities at all as a teacher they see evidence of all this around them every day.

What this book sets out to do, after a very brief reminder of the accepted, oft listed, advantages and disadvantages of small schools, is to suggest possible ways in which those strengths can be turned into positive educational gain and how the very real weaknesses, which only the most besotted will deny, can be met face to face and overcome. I believe in small schools and from years of teaching in them and inspecting them know that they can be places which offer children academic and social education of the highest possible quality; but I know also that they can trap children in a sterile and uninspiring classroom for four precious years of their young lives. Small isn't always beautiful, but it can be – everything will depend on how teachers grasp the opportunities offered and deal with the challenges which that very smallness creates.

Introduction

Small schools have special characteristics that set them a degree apart from larger schools and distinguish them as a discrete group wherever they are found. Their characteristics have been listed and debated many times and their strengths and weaknesses analysed in numerous publications. There is a considerable public and professional interest in these schools and the volume of published material reflects that interest.

It is not difficult to be enthused by the image of a small school. It often looks attractive, there is a feeling of security and a pleasing intimacy. It has a scale which relates to childhood, which is more easily encompassed by both child and adult. There is frequently a strong sense of community within the school and the school itself can relate closely to the community it serves and be accessible to it. All the children and usually their families are well known to the teachers and to each other. Little happens that the children are not aware of and, if need be, activities can involve all of them. It appears in fact a less turbulent and noisome place than its larger cousin; more like home, an altogether more relaxed, less hazardous, more natural staging post for our children on their journey towards a challenging adult world.

Such a view of small schools is, however, not the whole picture. A closer examination reveals a more complex and less cosy reality. Those who teach in small schools, or who are involved in their support, know that the very smallness that creates opportunities also creates problems. The intention of this book is to offer suggestions not only on maximising the opportunities offered but on dealing with these problems. In this introduction we remind ourselves briefly of what characteristics, what advantages and what disadvantages, distinguish a small school. No list, however, can fully convey the special atmosphere that pervades a small school or the satisfaction and pleasure that can come from teaching in one.

It is the simple fact that they are small that makes small schools different. They have small buildings, a small number of teachers, a small number of pupils and small budgets. If they are in the country they can be in isolated locations. They are frequently, but not always, linked to small but cohesive communities. From these facts flow the opportunities and the problems that characterise the small school. The most important of these are listed below.

Small pupil and staff numbers can mean the following:
- *Children receive more individual attention*, although this can be offset if the class is too large.
- *Teachers can get to know their children very well and often their families too*. Although it is important to guard against being over-protective and possessive of children, this is a major plus for small schools.
- *A more intimate and secure 'family'-like relationship is claimed with some justice*. It could be argued that this is a more natural setting for the education of small children than a larger institution.
- *Children are taught in classes which often have a wide spread of age and ability*. This poses real problems of organisation and class layout, but these can be overcome (as following chapters suggest). There are advantages in the need for children to develop skills in self-directed study, to lead groups of younger children, to take various classroom responsibilities as they grow older. It has been noted that children from small schools do tend to develop more responsible attitudes to work.
- *The continuous mixing with children of various ages can foster an ease of relationship with both older and younger children*. The children work together in project groups, play together, and age barriers mean much less. However, children do miss the classroom stimulation of a wide range of interests and opinion from a larger peer group and some social companionship from boys or girls of their own age. We shall see how co-operation between schools can help overcome this.
- *Teachers have a longer contact with one group of children*. This allows for continuity and improved matching of task to need.
- *Teachers enjoy a greater flexibility in organising the school day and the curriculum*. There are only one or two other teachers to share the hall, playing field, TV, computer, etc. Teachers can respond more quickly to new curricular demands or the need to introduce new methods, as there are fewer colleagues to reach consensus with.

- *There are fewer teacher specialist skills and a more limited range of interests to draw upon.* This is undeniable, but a sensible programme of in-service training to widen staff skills, close co-operation with other schools, a good peripatetic service and an imaginative use of the skills and interests of parents and members of the local community can go a long way to balance this.
- *Teachers receive less classroom support from a headteacher who has a full-time classroom responsibility.* But they do see a lot of him or her during break times and for much of the day. Co-operative and team teaching virtually negate this oft-suggested disadvantage. (As head of both large and small schools I found that administrative pressure and increased visitors made getting into classrooms just as difficult in my larger schools – and there were a far greater number of teachers to see!) The remedy lies with the LEA and the proper use of the most expensive professional in the school.
- *The stimulus of other classrooms and professional discussion is missed.* On a day-to-day basis this is true – but it is offset if the school works closely with others, makes the best use of appropriate in-service facilities and seizes every opportunity to get teachers into other schools.
- *Small budgets mean limited resources.* Weighted allowances, the help of supportive local communities and joint purchasing with neighbouring schools can do much to offset this.
- *Once purchased, children have much better access to expensive resources.* One or even two computers in a village classroom with two dozen children is not uncommon. Watch where the next generation of computer wizards will come from!
- *Isolation* can be very real for some small rural schools. It can be difficult for teachers to get to in-service centres. There are less frequent visits by advisers but there are fewer teachers to see when you get there. As a county adviser I probably knew the teachers in small schools better because of this. Co-operative school groups also help.

Small schools are often associated with small, cohesive communities, and thus may be supported in the following ways:
- There is a real and helpful interest in the school with support for fund raising and a greater participation in its day-to-day life. There is a willingness among people to become involved in what is more clearly seen as 'their' school. The use of special skills and interests among the community is described in chapter 6.
- Children have ready access to what is often a rich and varied community life of which their family is frequently already a part.

It is often a microcosm of a larger society with its traditions in music and dance, its customs and annual events, and in the occupations and leisure pursuits of the people.
- Small rural schools have access to natural environments rich in educational opportunity.
- School, curriculum and community can be linked in ways which encourage a sense of belonging and responsibility for the community in the children. It is a fact that villages are far less troubled by vandalism than large towns.

These, without elaboration, are some of the characteristics of small schools, the opportunities they offer and the problems they pose. The picture is more complex than these bare statements imply but one simple fact emerges: *whatever the balance of advantage and disadvantage is, children from small primary schools cope as readily with the next stage of their academic education as those from larger schools*. Secondary school teachers involved in a Department of the Environment and DES joint study 'The Social Effects of Rural Primary School Reorganisation, 1980/81' stated that in their view children from smaller primary schools were as well prepared academically as those from larger schools and generally possessed a better attitude to work.

Again, in an address to a conference on 'The Survival of the Small School' in 1979, Johnston stated 'The best and most recent evidence of pupil performance in our final external examinations in my own country [Scotland] shows that girls from sparsely populated areas do considerably better than girls from cities and boys do slightly better.'

It does not follow of course that the only reason for the success of these children is related solely to their probable attendance at a small primary school. Other factors such as lack of other distractions in a remote area may have encouraged attention to studies, but no one, to my knowledge, has yet come forward with proof that children from smaller primary schools fare less well in their secondary leaving examinations.

No doubt the advocates of larger schools and the enthusiasts for the smaller school will continue to declare the advantages or disadvantages outlined above. It is a personal belief that the strength of the small school lies in a more subtle factor which is less often, if ever, considered, and is concerned with the true nature of primary education.

It could be that primary education is essentially about the development of independent, critical thinking and the skills and basic knowledge that make this possible. The ability to think independently and to make necessary choices and decisions will depend on the individual's ability to assemble information, sort, validate and use it. This calls for specific learning skills of which numeracy and literacy are only two. It may well be that two good teachers can give this range of skills to children as effectively as seven teachers and that the wide variety of subject expertise offered by a larger staff is of less importance than is now frequently claimed. It could be also that the fostering of these investigative and decision-making skills takes place best when a sustained, trusting relationship between pupil and teacher develops. Such a relationship between tutor and student is often held as crucial in higher education. It may well be at the primary stage, when trust and confidence in adults is the base on which everything must be built, that this relationship is equally important. This prolonged contact between educated adult and child is a characteristic of small schools.

Any careful reading of the literature about small schools shows how difficult it is to assess the merits and demerits of them. What is seen as a source of strength to one observer is seen as weakness by another. Different perspectives affect judgements, while comment from those who are not trained observers can be very subjective. Smallness in itself, it seems, is no guarantee of success or failure. Primary education, however, takes place at a time in a child's development when relationships with adults are still paramount; the peer group has not yet taken over as the dominant moulder of attitudes, and the intimacy of a small school allows for a continuing close relationship between adult and child over a number of years.

That sustained relationship can be extremely fruitful and those who have taught in small schools will know how well the promise and problems of each child can be known to you. That knowledge can allow for just the right door of experience to be opened at just the right moment for that particular child. At the end of the day it is this opportunity to know the needs of the children you are teaching so well, and to respond to them, that makes small school teaching so enriching.

It is also the factor that puts great responsibility upon teachers in the small school and on the authority that appoints them. Just as the sustained relationship can be fruitful, it can as easily be harmful. It needs little imagination to conceive of the damage to a child's education and to that child's personal development which may result from a three- or four-year incarceration with an unimaginative, weak teacher. Some will see the main strength of the small school in its flexibility and the opportunity to involve the whole school in ventures of different kinds; others will deem the close links with the community as most important; yet others its informality and family atmosphere. The important thing is surely to be conscious of all these strengths and know how best to use them while being equally aware of weaknesses and how best these can be met and countered. The following chapters offer suggestions on this – no more.

1 Organising space

Far fewer small schools have been built since the Second World War than larger schools. This may be because the majority of small schools are in the countryside where the communities they serve have declined in population. In towns, on the other hand, rising populations have demanded new school building programmes. Frequently these new urban schools have led to the closing of smaller, ageing town schools. In the countryside where replacement has taken place it has often been by the creation of area schools and closure of those in surrounding villages.

Whatever the reason, the result has been that in many hundreds of small schools all over the country, teachers and pupils have to work in old and frequently inadequate buildings – often built in Victorian times or early in the 20th century. Very few small schools have been built in the last four decades. The older schools are often attractive to look at from the outside. Usually built of indigenous materials, they stand handsomely in the heart of the village, in the open countryside or in a more urban setting. Inside, these school buildings are far less inviting. High windows restrict any view of the outside world – such a distraction was considered undesirable by educationists of the day. Lofty ceilings make heating difficult, while large doorways and stone floors add to the unattractive interior.

No one, however, who has spent any time visiting small schools would deny that, unpromising though the basic provision may be, they are more often than not places of colour and full of vigorous life. This transformation from bleak Victorian classroom to warm, bright, modern school environment is almost entirely due to the succession of teachers who have had charge of these rooms. Bright curtains, carpets, new furniture and fresh paint have worked wonders in many a chill and depressing room.

All these improvements are welcome and of great benefit to the children; of this there can be little doubt. What is not so certain is whether teachers in making these improvements have always taken into full consideration the wide age and ability range of the children they will be teaching. Certainly in any primary school catering for 5- to 11-year-olds with four or fewer staff, this range will exist. This must in turn make demands upon the way the classroom is arranged.

Class and school organisation are looked at in more detail in chapter 2, but mixed age and ability teaching has a number of characteristics which should have an effect on class layout and it will be helpful to state the most important of these at this point.

Mixed age and ability teaching will call for the following:
  (a) Children to be taught in small groups within the class.
  (b) Children not being taught will have to be engaged in self-directed activity of some sort.
  (c) These self-directed activities will probably be very diverse in nature and a wide range of activities is likely to be going on in the classroom at the same time.

These simple facts should have important implications for the layout. There are other implications, of course – for teaching style, methods of evaluation, resources and much else – but here we are concerned with the effect on room layout of teaching a mixed-ability/wide age range class.

If there is to be small-group teaching within the classroom then there is a need for an area which allows for the teacher and some of the children to gather in a group with the least possible interruption from the rest of the class. At the same time the teacher will need to have an eye to the other activities going on in the room.

The children not being directly taught will be busy with a variety of self-directed activities, planned with the teacher but carried out independently as individuals or in small groups. These activities are likely to demand the provision of activity and resource bays, including places for quiet study.

The room will also have to allow for the teacher to draw together the whole class for discussion or instruction when this is appropriate. There will be other times when the whole class will be engaged in workshop-type activities and the room layout will have to take this into account.

The suggested layouts that follow try to reflect these basic assumptions about the nature of mixed-ability/wide age range teaching. They are not exhaustive by any means, but they do depart quite markedly from the more traditional arrangements that one finds in many classrooms where such teaching has to take place.

The first layout (Figure 1) is for a single classroom, in this case a junior room. Figure 2 illustrates an infants room. Many infants teachers will find this layout unexceptional and many would say they have long led the field in setting out their rooms to reflect their teaching needs and the style of the children's learning. These layouts for single classrooms are applicable in any reasonably sized room. Some suggestions are made for easing the problems created by rooms too small to fully implement these ideas.

Where two or more teachers have agreed to work together in co-operation and to share space and plan their work together, then the possibility of offering a much greater variety in layout is increased. The later illustrations (Figures 3, 4, 7 and 9) show possible layouts in two-, three- and four-teacher schools for such co-operative teaching. Many teachers do work in close co-operation with colleagues and share many activities together but too seldom give enough consideration to an arrangement of their rooms which would facilitate such co-operation. The suggestions are kept within the most common building patterns encountered in smaller schools but most can be adapted to other designs with a little imagination. The organisation of the school day, pupil groupings and teaching styles is discussed in chapter 2.

Making the best use of the classroom space is very important, but many teachers are also creative in their use of other available space. In the past many of our village schools had to cater for larger numbers of children and thus cloakrooms, wide passages and even empty classrooms are sometimes available. Often alongside the school stands the school house and some authorities have taken these into use as part of the teaching area.

Junior room

The suggested room layout for a junior room (Figure 1) pre-supposes that a teacher faced with a class of wide ability and age range will follow the most common practice in such a situation and divide the class into groups. (The Welsh Office Survey No. 6 of 1978 states that 95% of teachers covered by this survey of small schools in Wales grouped their children for most studies and activities.) Groups can be arranged according to ability, age, interest or common goal. It is suggested that teachers should be flexible in their use of grouping type. The deciding factor must always be the pupil need that has to be met. At any particular time any one of the above group types may meet that pupil need: at another time that need may be better and more economically met by the whole class being brought together; and at yet another time each child may work or

Teaching in the smaller school

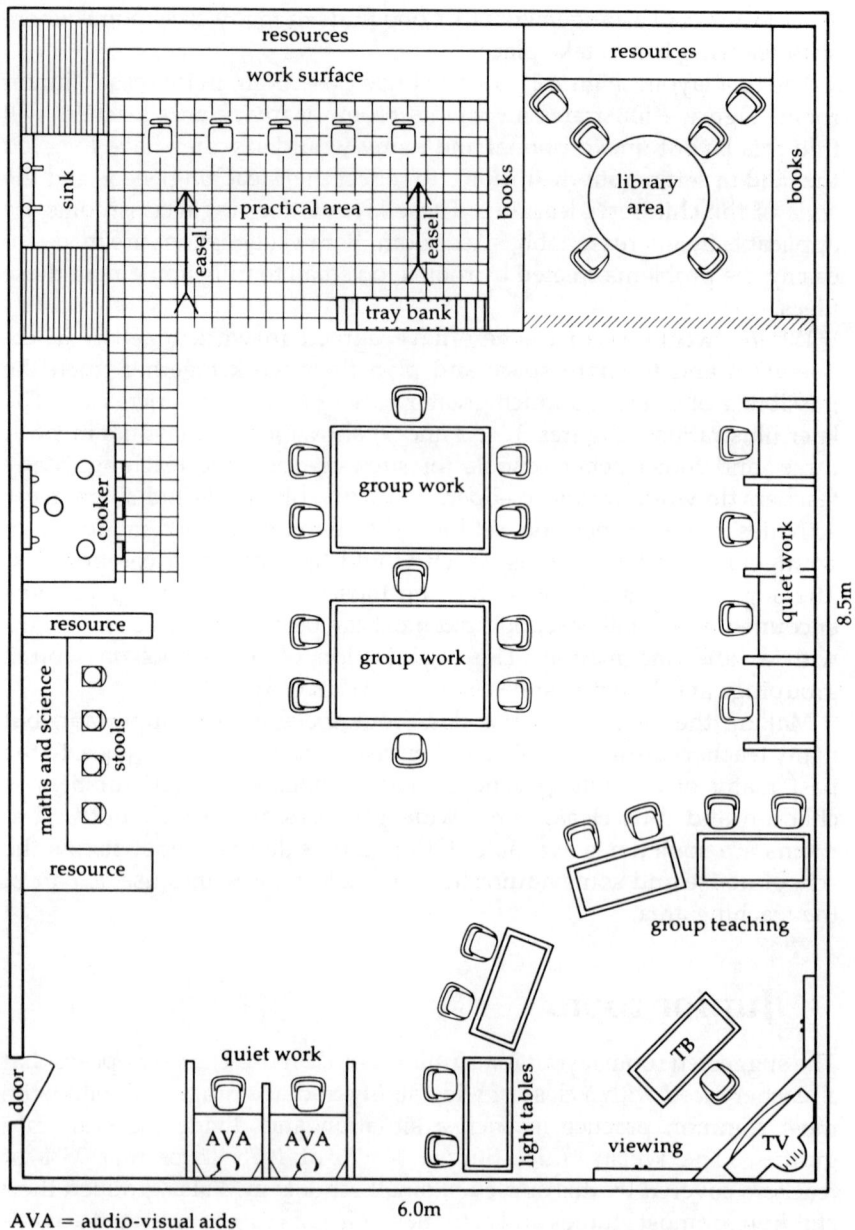

AVA = audio-visual aids
TB = teacher base

1. Suggested layout for a junior room for 30 pupils of wide-ranging abilities and ages where mixed-ability teaching is called for.

be taught individually. The room layout suggested allows for a diversity of groupings and activities:
- The group teaching area allows the teacher to work with a small group while still having a good view of the room.
- The variety of quiet study and practical work bays caters for a range of individual and group activities.
- When the teacher needs to address the whole class there is a seat and writing surface for each child.

Arranging the work for a mixed age/ability class in such a room as this is considered in detail in chapter 2.

Infants room

A layout for an infants room, where the teacher has to deal with a three-year age range and a wide ability span, is illustrated in Figure 2. Much will depend on the size and shape of the room but there are activity areas which should be included if at all possible. This arrangement includes the following:
- A language bay which is also the class gathering area and the teacher base. This area should be carpeted.
- A floor play area with constructional toys. This is also carpeted.
- A maths and science resource area and bench for older infants.
- A sand and clay area – close to an outside door if possible.
- A role-play area with facilities for imaginative play.
- A water tray and suitably tiled floor area for art and messier activities.
- Group work tables.
- Display boards, interest tables and stands.

The nature of this type of infants class with its wide age range will call for both group and individual teaching. The organisational pattern favoured varies from class to class. While some teachers will emphasise groups, perhaps using a rotating system with groups visiting activity areas in turn (the carousel system), others will favour a greater emphasis on individual programmes for each child. The majority are likely to be found somewhere between the two.

We look in the next chapter at actual examples of the carousel system in action in a two-teacher infants unit and at a single infants classroom using a mixture of group and individual teaching.

6   *Teaching in the smaller school*

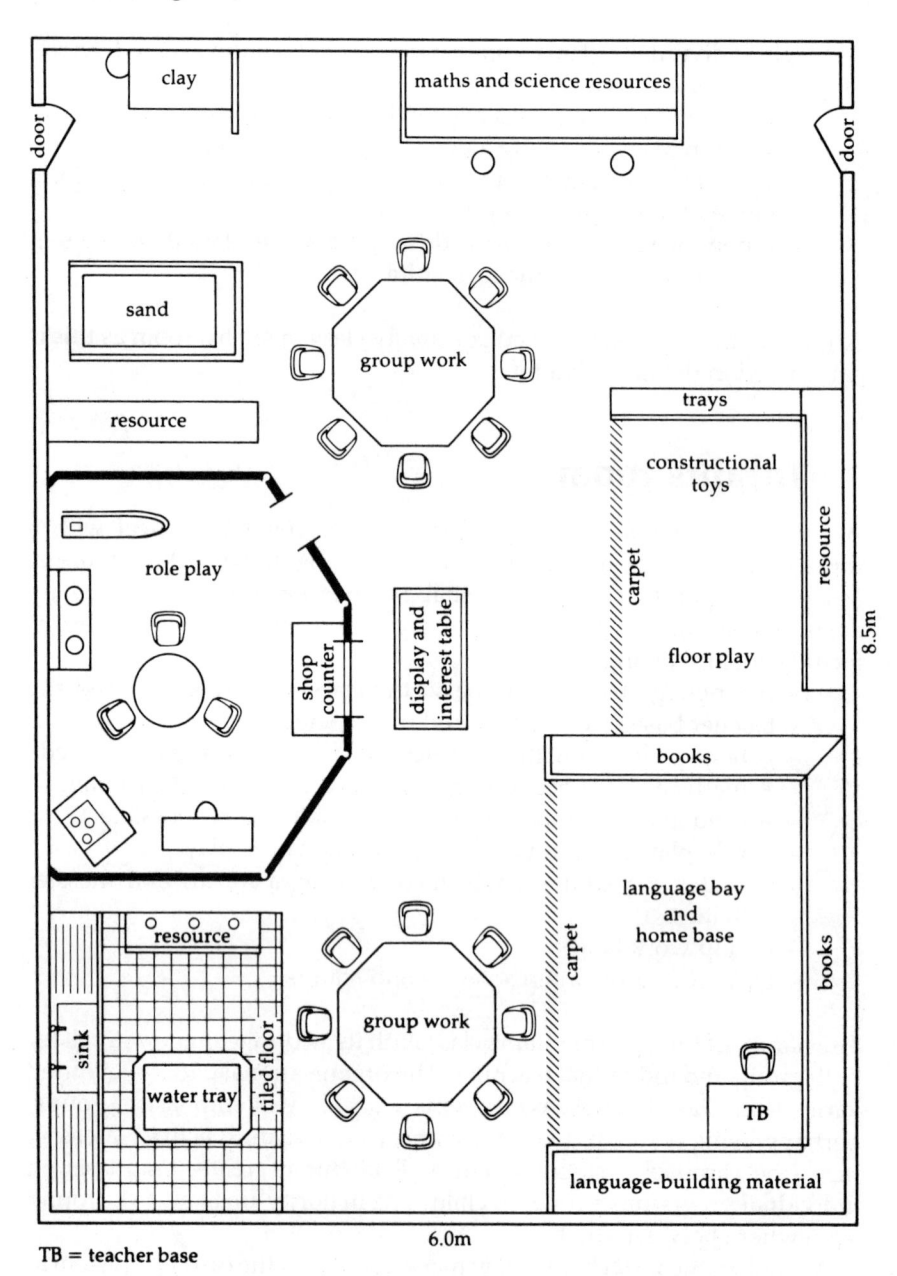

TB = teacher base

2. Suggested layout for an infants room for 25 pupils with an age range from reception to top infants (7+) – a three-year age and ability span.

Teaching together

The layouts for junior and infants rooms which have been suggested can of course be modified to suit the size and shape of the available space as long as the basic concepts are adhered to. There is an assumption, however, that the teachers working in these rooms will be working in separated classes, spending most of the school day alone with their children. However, in two-, three- and four-teacher schools there is often an opportunity to work in much closer co-operation with colleagues, sharing space, time and skills. When teachers do come together to teach co-operatively then they need to set out their rooms to facilitate this teaching together.

We look first at a two-teacher school, with one infants and one junior teacher. Such schools are the most common type of two-teacher small school and may have up to 50 children in them or as few as 25 or even less. If the two teachers have decided to regard themselves as jointly responsible for all the children rather than having strictly separated class responsibilities, then this implies shared space. A possible format for this is considered below.

The three-teacher school is likely to have two junior teachers and an infants teacher. A completely open school would link all three classrooms, but within the constraints of the buildings it is more likely that only two of the classrooms can be joined. In the majority of rural schools it was common to have a screen between two of the classrooms and it is this that offers the opportunity to set out two rooms for some type of co-operative teaching. Where this takes place the most likely link is between the two junior teachers although circumstances may bring infants and lower juniors together.

The two-teacher school

The two-teacher school illustrated in Figure 3 has the common basic design of such schools: a rectangular shell divided by a screen, the infants room usually being slightly smaller than the junior room. The screen has been folded back but is retained and the rooms are laid out to facilitate co-operation between the two teachers.

The two members of staff have decided that they will look upon themselves as having some responsibility for teaching all the children in the school rather than as having responsibility only for the junior or infants classes – although they will remain in general charge of their own pupil age group. Once this decision is taken then it is sensible to lay out the rooms in ways that facilitate this co-operation.

There is a large practical area open to all the children and a shared library. There is a maths and science bay which infants as well as juniors

AVA = audio-visual aids
TB = teacher base

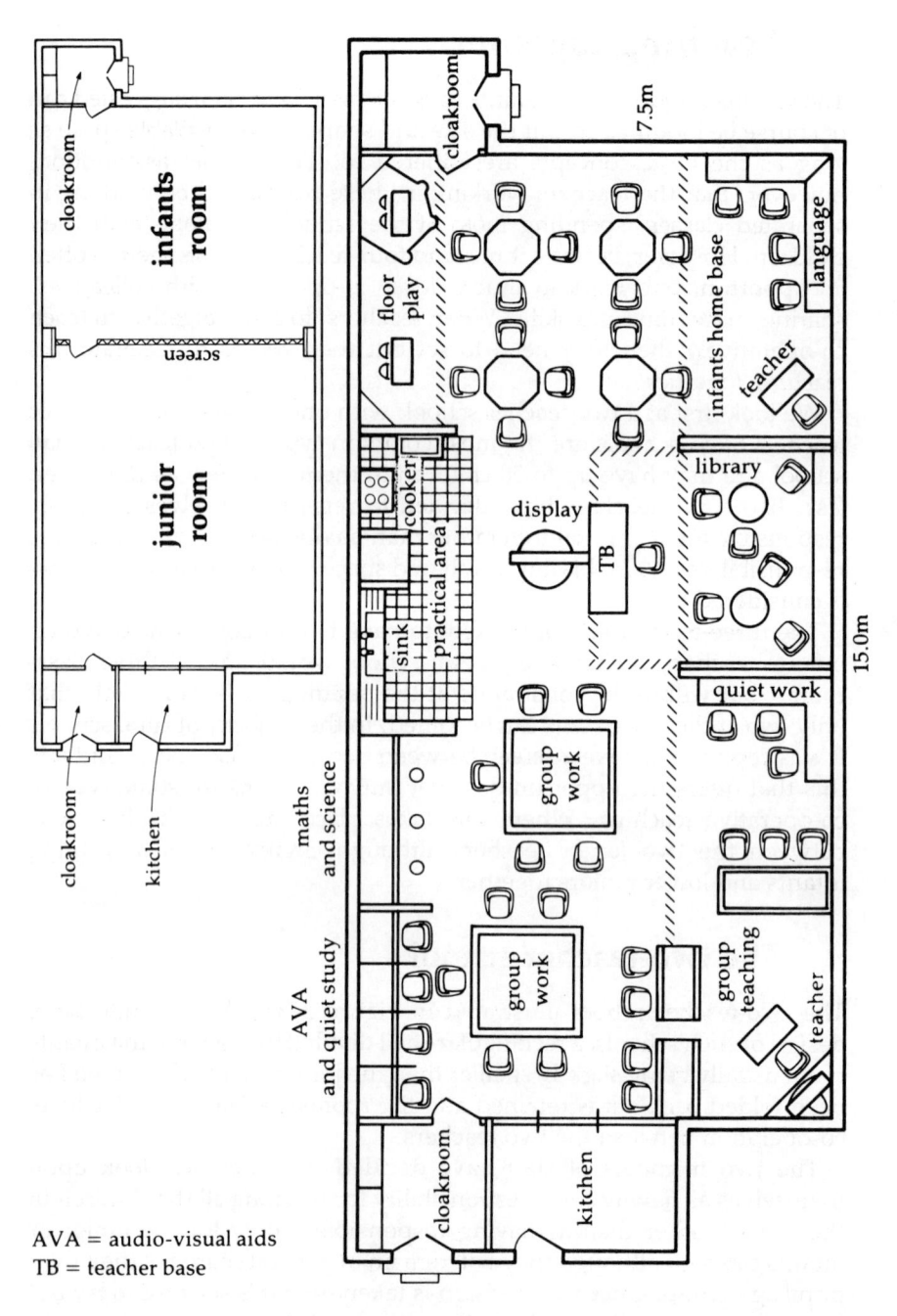

3. Two-teacher infants/junior unit for co-op-erative teaching: an alternative to separated classrooms in a small school. The most common design for a two-teacher school is a recentagle divided by a screen.

can use. A junior group teaching area and an infants home base for gathering with the teacher are provided.

The arrangement of the room enables the teachers to work together in a number of different ways.

(a) The movement of children from infants to junior area is simple and allows for children to move to groups on either side as need demands. It would for instance be simple for an able infant to join a junior group for maths or a slower-learning first-year junior to make use of the infants word-building sets.

(b) If the infants teacher wishes to have some time alone with the reception group, or the junior teacher with the 11+ leavers, or if any group needs uninterrupted time, this can be planned with the other teacher supervising the remaining children. Teacher bases are placed to allow for such group work and for general supervision of the whole area.

(c) The linked classrooms make it easier for the two teachers to be flexible in the way in which they form their groups, mixing children from both classes if the interest of the pupils demands it.

(d) The resources from both classes continue to be available to both groups of children. For example, junior books are readily available to the able reader from the infants group, while language and maths apparatus from the infants room remains available to the slower-learning junior.

(e) It is easier for the two teachers to discuss and monitor the progress of children through the school. The infants teacher continues to have contact during the day with the children who have moved to the junior group, is able to observe them, has access to their work and can comment on it.

(f) The planning and implementation of projects or thematic work together is made simpler because of the ongoing contacts that the teachers enjoy.

(g) The special skills and interests of both teachers are more readily available to all the children more of the time.

(h) An insecure child may benefit from the continued presence of a teacher with whom he or she may have a greater empathy. The danger of strained relationships between a pupil and teacher who find it difficult to relate but have to be together for up to four years is eased.

(i) The arrangement of the rooms allows for infant and junior groups to work separately if need demands. Carpets and well-placed display stands facilitate this, reducing noise and making visual breaks.

Suggestions for organising the school day are given in chapter 2.

The three-teacher school

The design of the school illustrated in Figure 5 (a) – a long rectangle divided into three rooms by a wall and a screen – is common and based on a large number of actual schools. In such schools there are normally two junior and one infants trained teachers. The school is normally organised into an infants class, lower juniors with perhaps a few older infants, depending on the age distribution, and an upper junior class. To facilitate liaison the two junior classes are often situated next to one another.

In such circumstances it is possible to increase the amount of co-operation between the two junior classes and this is made easier if the classrooms are set out in ways which reflect the teachers' intention to work more closely together. Much will depend on the degree to which the staff wish to take their co-operative teaching.

In the layouts suggested the first (b) assumes that the teachers:
- wish to share library, practical facilities and certain other resources;
- will cross-group the children where they think this helpful;
- will co-operate in the development of projects and thematic work;
- will share their special areas of expertise; and
- will evaluate and discuss children's progress and generally work closely together. However they will still see themselves as based in their lower or upper junior rooms and will do most of their teaching there with their own class.

In the second example (c) the teachers have gone further than this. They have decided to share responsibility for all the junior children and to teach them together (Figure 4). The rooms have been laid out to reflect this decision. One teacher remains the registration teacher for the lower juniors and the other for the older children but the planning of the school day is done jointly and either teacher may be working with either age group during the day. The advantages that the teachers seek by this close co-operation are set out below.

(a) *Flexible groupings* Groups can be formed to answer the various needs of the pupils. For example:
- The nature of the group can respond to ability, age, interest or common goal. Members of the group can be drawn from all four junior age groups. The enlarged number of children makes the formation of interest and common goal groups easier.
- The size of the group can range from all the junior children brought together, through class-sized groups and smaller groups to one-to-one tuition.
- The flexibility of grouping is made possible by one of the

teachers supervising a large group doing self-directed work and thus releasing the other teacher to work with a smaller group without interruption. Such sharing calls for careful planning but is used successfully in schools following a pattern of team or co-operative teaching.

(b) *Use of special skills* Special skills or the interests of either teacher remain more readily available to all the children.

(c) *Discussion of professional matters* Joint planning, implementation and evaluation of the children's work encourages professional dialogue and development.

(d) *More flexible use of available space* The shared space makes it possible to create a greater variety of areas and thus provide for a range of activities from quiet individual study to practical work in groups of varying sizes.

(e) *A wider range of resources* There need be no duplication of resources as there might be in two separate classrooms. A greater variety of library books, audio-visual aids, educational equipment and materials becomes possible.

(f) *Assessment of children's progress* Assessment of academic progress and personal growth needs is aided by discussion between the teachers.

4. Two teachers working in co-operation.

12 *Teaching in the smaller school*

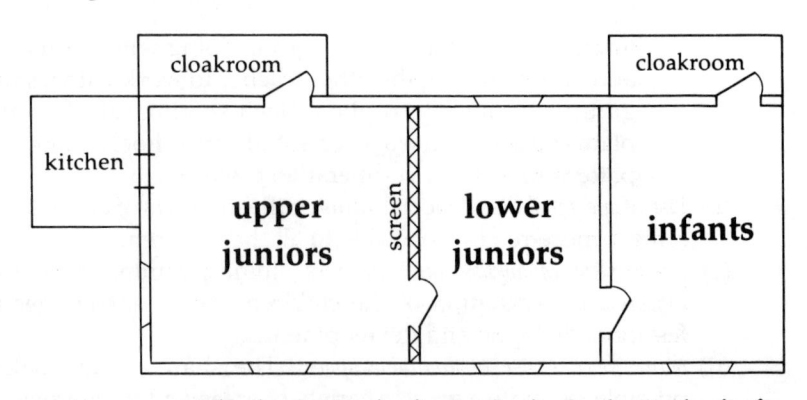

UDT = upper display trolley (low cupboard on castors with vertical display surface on back)

TB = teacher base

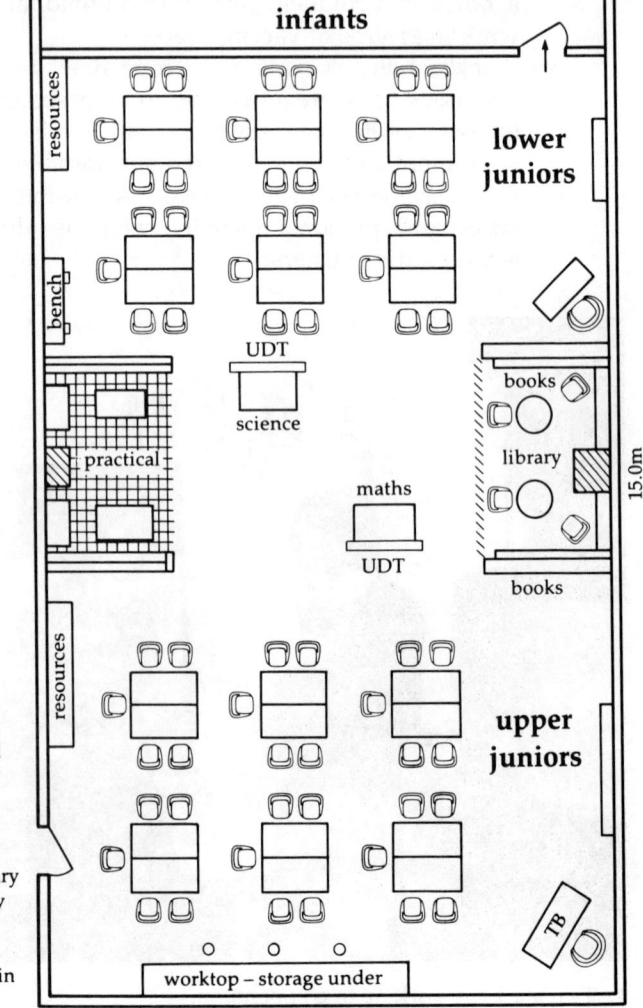

The two junior classes, screen folded back and space arranged for limited co-operative teaching; e.g. shared maths and science resources; shared library and practical area; easy access to allow for flexible interclass grouping. Classes retain their own form areas.

Organising space 13

infants room

small TV

TB = teacher base

group teaching

tall cupboards

practical area

screen – part closed

bookshelves

carpet

display

stools

work surface

maths and science resource

TB

15.0m

display

books

CB

library

quiet room

study carrels

teacher

7.5m

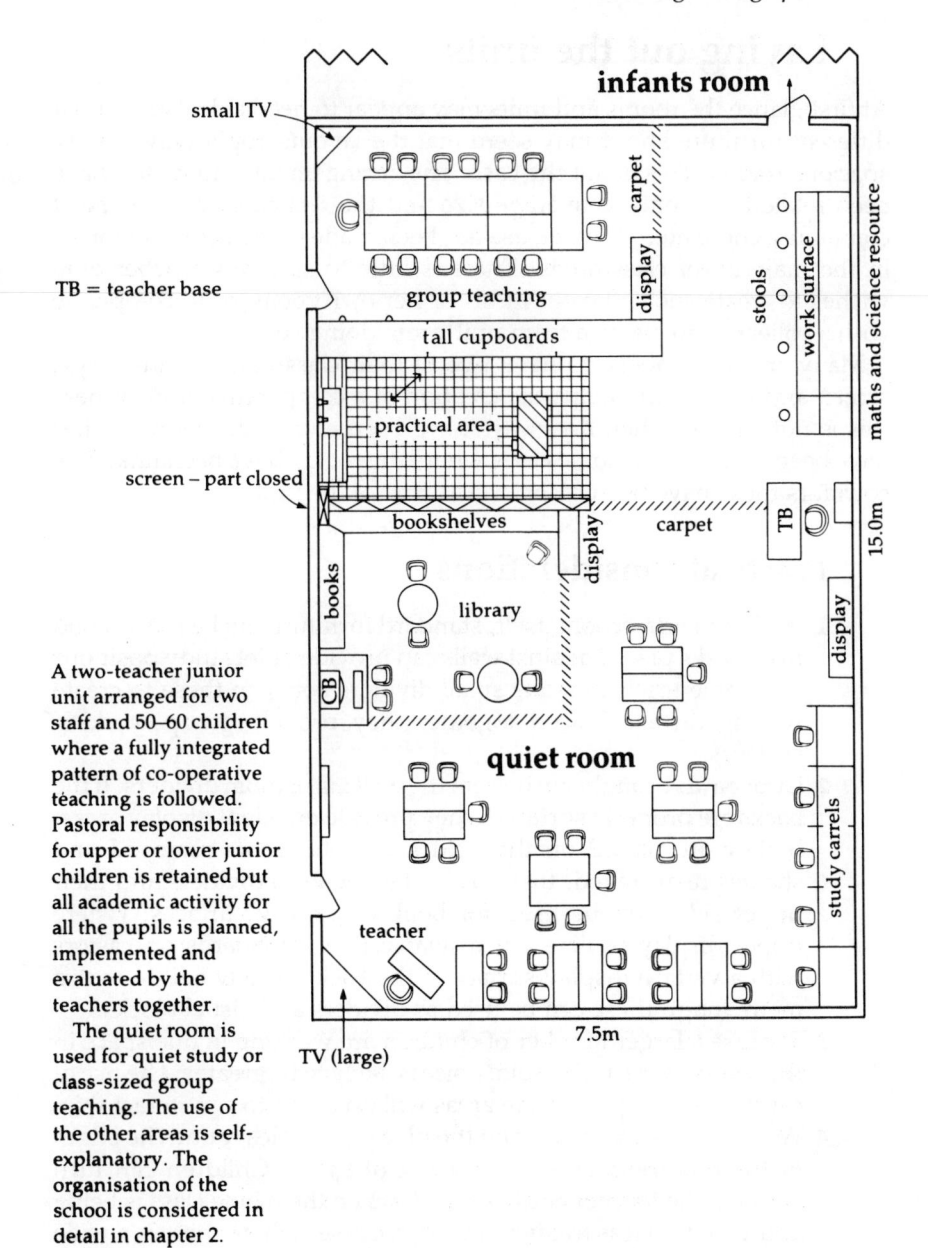

TV (large)

A two-teacher junior unit arranged for two staff and 50–60 children where a fully integrated pattern of co-operative teaching is followed. Pastoral responsibility for upper or lower junior children is retained but all academic activity for all the pupils is planned, implemented and evaluated by the teachers together.

The quiet room is used for quiet study or class-sized group teaching. The use of the other areas is self-explanatory. The organisation of the school is considered in detail in chapter 2.

5. Teaching together: the three-teacher school
(a) A common design for the three-teacher school – a divided rectangle.
(b) The two-teacher junior unit – limited co-operative teaching.
(c) The two-teacher junior unit – arranged for fully integrated co-operative teaching.

Laying out the units

At first glance the rooms and units may appear to need a deal of extra or different furniture and it may seem that the layouts apply only to very spacious rooms. This is not the case. The arrangements illustrated have been related to rooms of average size and the rectangular shape most commonly encountered, while use has been made of the furniture found in the majority of classrooms. There is little to stop any teacher who wishes to create such a layout in his or her own room (or to co-operate with a colleague to create a team unit) from doing so.

Many smaller schools do have two of their classrooms divided by a screen and this greatly helps the creation of a co-operative unit. Where this is not the case then doorways have been enlarged, linking arches have been made and in some cases where the rooms have been linked by corridors these have been embraced as part of the unit.

Practical considerations

1 Within the classroom itself, standard furniture can be put to good use. Desks placed against walls can provide quiet study positions and some teachers make small dividers between these to create writing carrels. Placed together they provide group working surfaces.
2 Cupboards brought away from the wall make room dividers. If the backs are properly surfaced, they provide excellent display areas. If they are placed on their sides and the doors removed and shelves re-arranged, they can make low-level dividers and their upper sides can be used for book or display surfaces. Where upper display trolleys are available (low cupboards on castors with a vertical display surface at the back, usually a little over a metre long), these can be used as dividers and visual blocks.
3 Because a larger number of children are working in one space in the co-operative units, total noise is likely to be greater. The use of carpets in the appropriate areas will do much to counteract this.
4 Where rooms are small then the placing of tables round the edges of the classroom creates a feeling of space. Children can turn towards the teacher easily enough when the whole class is being addressed – a less frequent event in classes where there is a wide range of age and ability, which is usually the case in small schools.
5 In mixed age/ability classes there is usually a good deal of self-directed individual work. Where this involves writing or quiet study the use of writing carrels is very helpful. These can be made by placing ordinary school desks or tables against the wall

and making small dividers about 30cm to 45cm high to separate the positions at desktop level. This is an aid to concentration as there is less visual distraction. Children see adults using such carrels in libraries and other places and enjoy the change from the open desk.
6 The layout of the practical area can include easels which are left standing ready for use; suitable surfaces and storage for clay work; a bench and access to a sink. It is a great help if the floor of this area is surfaced with non-slip vinyl or tiles.
7 The arrangement of the group teaching bay in the two-teacher junior unit brings the children around a large table formed by bringing a number of small tables together. This is a space-saver where room is at a premium. It also introduces children to another seating arrangement, the nature of which encourages discussion with the teacher and the rest of the group, discussion obviously being a very important part of group teaching.
8 It is helpful to have maths and science equipment accessible on open shelves and above a working surface where any practical activity can be carried out.
9 The group teaching bay is placed away from the quiet room. Experience has shown that discussion from the group teaching bay causes less distraction to children following a practical activity than it would to children reading and writing in the quiet room.

A final comment

We have looked at ways in which classrooms can be set out to help teachers in meeting the challenge of a class of wide age and ability range. We have looked briefly also at the setting out of rooms for co-operative teaching and what this can mean in enlarging the variety of facilities and resources.

What we should also remember is that because of their size small schools allow for the whole place at times to be transformed into a totally different environment which can be both stimulating and productive. Over the years I have walked into schools which had become Elizabethan galleons, village streets, Roman towns and Indian encampments. I well remember one school that had become a jungle and was ablaze with tropical birds, flowers, vegetation and animals. When you entered one entirely enclosed part of the jungle a waterfall started up and tropical bird song began.

As a motivation and support for projects, this type of transformation can be very effective – it also relieves the tedium of walking into the same classroom perhaps for four years. Motivation is a large part of the game in the education of young children; teachers, I sometimes think, enjoy it just as much. It can certainly lift a project into new dimensions and may well incidentally lift the school caretaker into new dimensions as she struggles to clean up the Amazon. But schools were made for children and if it provides a test for personnel management skills, so be it.

It is noticeable in visits to many schools that teachers who are bold in other ways are hesitant in making fundamental changes to the layout of their rooms. But the challenge of very wide age and ability ranges does make it important to rethink traditional arrangements. The layouts suggested, especially those for co-operative teaching and the junior room, may seem unusual but they do try to reflect the nature of the classes we are likely to face in a small school.

2 Teaching mixed age and ability classes

The greatest challenge facing teachers in small schools is that of organising effectively a class which includes children covering a very wide range of ages and abilities. In a two-teacher school the junior class may include children of 7 years of age to 11 years of age with abilities which match those of a 5-year-old or a 13-year-old. The infants teacher may be faced with a reception group which includes children better suited to a nursery and bright 7-year-olds well able to hold their own with older juniors. Faced with this range of age and ability within one class, teachers have to examine the way in which they organise their school day and the teaching style they use with the same imagination and care with which they need to approach the layout of their rooms. Even in schools of three or four teachers there can still be wide age/ability ranges to cater for.

It has been suggested that the variety of space available in small schools can be improved by teachers co-operating closely and sharing space. In the same way, meeting wide age and ability ranges among the children can be eased by close co-operation and the sharing of time and skills by the teachers involved. This type of co-operation will be looked at in some detail, but the task facing the teacher who works for the most part alone in a small-school classroom is also considered. Before looking at either of these alternatives, it may be helpful to clarify some of the problems that have to be faced in mixed-ability classrooms and establish some general principles in seeking their solution.

The problems have to be met whether a teacher works alone or closely with a colleague and whether teaching areas are shared or closed off. They stem from the basic fact that the needs of children of different ages and at different stages of their development are not always the same and

18   Teaching in the smaller school

Pupil's educational need

Activity by pupil to meet that need

Factors to be considered by the teacher in constructing that activity

What	What the activity teaches – skills, facts, concepts, attitudes to learning; to meet a physical, social or personal growth need
When	When the activity is to take place, overall time given to it, duration of session, frequency of session, whether teacher or pupil decides timing
Where	Home base, quiet study area, practical area, workshop, hall, outside the school, etc.
How	The learning method used – direct teaching, teacher-prescribed activity, self-directed activity
With whom	The activity to be carried out by the pupil alone, in a small group, class-sized or larger group; the nature of the group decided by age, achievement, interest or common goal
With what	The books, materials or equipment needed for the activity

---

6. Responding to educational needs.

often cannot be met by teaching them the same thing at the same time and in the same way. A teacher's task is to identify the educational needs of each child and to respond to that need in appropriate ways. It will call for a whole range of decisions to be made, as Figure 6 illustrates. The factors listed in this chart are but a few of those taken into consideration by any teacher when a pupil is being set an activity to follow. Usually the decisions are made quickly and often without conscious consideration of all these factors. Nevertheless, all of them are involved. The principle which is important in terms of the teacher of a mixed age/ability class is that different needs call for different combinations of responses and it is a mistake to be trapped into a uniform response. Flexibility has to be the key when the nature of a class presents a particularly wide variety of educational needs among its pupils. There is no one way to meet the demands of such a class; all the options have to stay open.

Grouping the children

A whole range of possible grouping presents itself. At times the complete school may be brought together; more frequently the group will be the class or groups formed within it. The pupils may at other times work in pairs or individually and the nature of all these groupings will relate to the need being responded to. The nature of the mixed-ability class can at times cause teachers to rely too heavily on individually prescribed work and neglect the economy and the merits of group or class teaching. It may be helpful to outline briefly the activities which can be undertaken effectively in these various groupings.

Larger than class-sized groups

Most frequently this is the whole school at assembly, but such groups can also be formed to listen to visiting speakers, to watch educational television or for certain types of games session. Teachers working in co-operative units will often supervise a large group of pupils doing mainly self-directed or prescribed work while a colleague has a small group for direct teaching and discussion.

Class-sized groups

Class teaching is far less widely used than it was a few decades ago, even when pupils in the class are of similar age and attainment. However, if the material being taught is suitable, it remains an effective and economical method of teaching, has the advantage of giving the class cohesion and allows for the interplay of a variety of opinions. A class with a very wide mix of age and ability will make it less likely that teachers are able to use this approach so often, but it is still appropriate on some occasions and should not be neglected. In a class whose nature means that children must frequently work in small groups or independently and without the immediate presence of the teacher, there is great value in re-establishing those pupil/teacher links by bringing the class together as a unit. Infants teachers do this at regular intervals throughout the day, recognising the need – among other things – to reinforce the security and confidence of young children.

The class will of course often be involved in working on the same topic or subject area but there will also be occasions when the class can actually be taught as a whole. Among these occasions will be the following:
   – Oral and written work when the emphasis is on the expression of opinion, justification, description or narrative and the response can be at a level appropriate to the individual pupil.

- Language or mathematics when certain basic concepts and skills which need regular reinforcement and repetition throughout the primary phase are being taught.
- Initiating and motivating thematic project work as well as ongoing explanation, summarising and concluding this work.
- Reading stories, enjoying verse, singing and making music, physical education, some types of two- and three-dimensional art and certain other practical activities.

There will be other areas of the curriculum, particularly where the emphasis is on motivation and introduction, when work with the whole class will precede a move to more detailed work with individuals or small groups.

Smaller groups

Much of the teaching in a class of mixed age and ability can be most successfully carried out with small groups formed for a whole range of purposes. Their nature may relate to the members' ages, achievement level, ability, potential, interest or common goal. Rigid grouping which settles a child into a particular group for all teaching purposes, whether it is formed on the basis of age or achievement, does not in the end enable the teacher to respond to the varying needs which each child has. To remain flexible over grouping so that each group formed most closely responds to the particular needs of the children in that group at that particular time has to be recommended.

It is convenient to examine the purposes of these smaller groups under headings which indicate their general nature.

Achievement groups

These are useful when the subject is essentially linear or sequential (mathematics is a good example of such a subject). However, not only in mathematics, but also in some types of language work, science, acquiring certain motor skills and on many other occasions, it is helpful to gather children of similar levels of achievement into the same group. These need not be permanent groups or identified too prominently; indeed to do so could introduce the danger of less able children losing confidence in their own ability. The dangers of streaming children are well known and few would advocate the divisions of children in a mixed-ability class into permanent, all-embracing achievement or ability groups. That is not what is suggested here. The children will be brought together in different types of group for a variety of purposes, among which the achievement group is only one. To ignore its usefulness, used wisely, is to neglect a very valuable teaching strategy.

Common goal groups

The pupils in these groups need not be of similar levels of achievement, age or ability. Such groups are most likely to be formed for project work in social or environmental studies when the class is divided into groups to follow some particular topic within the project's main theme. In forming these groups the teacher may be as concerned with the children developing such qualities as responsibility and tolerance, acquiring learning skills or fostering enthusiasms and interests, as with absorbing a discrete body of facts. Common goal groups are formed for many other purposes where the mixture of age, ability or achievement does not affect the satisfactory reaching of that goal. These groups are very important within the context of a mixed age/ability class. The construction of activities for such groups is considered in greater detail in the next chapter.

Interest groups

These are formed when there is value in bringing children with a similar interest together. For example, the opportunity often arises in project work when children are given a choice of groups, each following a particular theme. Music, two- and three-dimensional art, drama, hobbies and games are also areas where pupils develop specific interests and gain from a chance to share their enthusiasms with like-minded friends.

Age groups

Children will often be grouped with others of the same age; indeed, in some mixed-age classes, teachers age-group pupils for the major part of their work. This can be an error and lead to underperformance or stress. One of the advantages of having a mixed age/ability class is that children can work, as appropriate, with children who may have similar interests, abilities and needs regardless of age. Often need and response will create groups of children of the same age, but that grouping should be because of need and not because of age. There will be times when age groups do need to be drawn together, for example the 11+ leavers will have much in common to investigate relevant to their move to secondary education, but using age as the main criterion is unwise.

The challenge to teachers in using small groups of these and other types for direct teaching, discussion, prescribed or self-directed activity of all kinds, is organising the class in ways that free the teacher to work without interruption with one particular group. It will help a great deal if the classroom is set out appropriately and co-operative teaching with a colleague can do much to ease the problem, but it is careful classroom organisation which above all holds the key to the successful management of a mixed age/ability class.

One fundamental distinction which is little discussed, but which is very important, is that between pupil activity which demands a teacher's full attention and that which demands only light supervision. It is only by ensuring that some groups are pursuing activities that demand little of the teacher's attention that the teacher can be sure of having reasonably uninterrupted time with other groups. This seems the most obvious of statements but it is not uncommon to find a mixed-ability class, perhaps with an age-span of as much as four years, with all the pupils simultaneously working on a subject in which pupils frequently need teacher-help, for example mathematics. Whether the teacher arranges the children's work individually or in groups, the chances are that under these circumstances this demand for attention will result in an unproductive line of children at the teacher's desk. Unfortunately some teachers appear to accept this line as inevitable and cease to look for solutions.

The solution to this problem lies to some extent at least in ensuring that not all the children are following an activity which is so demanding of the teacher's attention. This means in the first place examining very carefully which activities demand close involvement and which less. It is not a simple matter of subject division because clearly some activities within a single subject demand more attention from the teacher than others. Even within a subject such as mathematics this is so.

It lies with each teacher to decide from his or her own experience which activities in the classroom demand their undivided attention and those where the children are able to work in more self-directed ways, and then aim for a balance, at appropriate times, between the two. In a mixed age/ability class the achievement of this balance will be crucial in the avoidance of impossible demands upon the teacher and unproductive waiting for the children.

If a teacher has organised the class to give a balance between teacher-demanding and less demanding activities then it follows that those pupils not directly involved with the teacher will be working in a self-directed way in groups or individually. The group work may involve discussion and co-operative activity within the group to achieve the goals set; on the other hand the group may be an organisational convenience for setting similar work to a number of children who then work individually. In other cases the teacher may not group children but aim to programme work for each child individually.

Individualised learning

Whether an educational activity is initiated in a class or in a smaller grouping, more frequently than not it results in a task carried out individually by the pupil. There is, however, a difference between tasks resulting from work initiated in a group and that set specifically for an individual. Many teachers faced by a class of wide-ranging age and ability attempt to overcome this disparity by programming work for each child individually. In some cases the bulk of the basic skill work of the children is carried out following a system of individual programming.

On the surface this is an attractive teaching strategy and responds to belief in the importance of child-centred education, of children working at their own speed and even deciding for themselves the order in which they tackle each prescribed task. The teacher appears as consultant ready to clarify the new concept as it appears and ensuring that the programme undertaken is properly meeting the child's educational need. Unfortunately unless numbers are very small, such individual tutoring is extremely difficult to operate successfully.

Teachers who are unable to produce and supervise an individually devised programme for each child by themselves, often turn to the profusion of attractively presented commercial card and textbook sets of graded exercises, supplemented perhaps by their own teacher-produced work cards. Pupils are introduced to these at appropriate levels and work their way through the course. The results of a heavy reliance on this system are not always happy. The number of children involved is frequently too large and some or all of the following may happen:

- Unless the number of children is very small, teachers have only a short time to discuss new concepts or processes with each child.
- Because of the pressure on the teacher, the card or textbook is relied upon to introduce a new concept or process. This is a dangerous assumption to make with young children, who usually need exposition and clarification to learn thoroughly.
- If there is failure to grasp the new process, then a return to swell the line at the teacher's desk is more than likely. It also means that the pupil/teacher contact is too frequently made at the point of breakdown rather than success. While it is proper for teachers to fill the role of helper when things go wrong, it is equally important that they are seen by pupils as partners in the successful exploration of new ideas and pupil/teacher contacts as preliminaries to success.
- The increased likelihood of failure which can result from inadequate initial explanation is discouraging and eventually harmful to the pupil's self-image and confidence.
- In order to build in some success, relieve pressure on the teacher and keep the children busy, there is a tendency for the task undertaken to become less challenging and not to promote genuine development. Indeed it has been observed in a number of reports that these tasks can become so routine as to have little real value.

- Although children following this pattern of work mingle with other pupils they can in fact be working in isolation for long periods of the day. The stimulation which comes with group or class discussion is lost.

This is not to imply that working alone, whether it be following a programme devised by the teacher or pursuing a personal interest in a self-directed way, is not of value; it remains one of the most effective work patterns for children in the mixed age/ability class, but teachers have to be alert to the dangers which lie in attempting to base too much of the children's activity on that pattern.

In mathematics in particular it is common to find children working individually through card- or textbook-based programmes with a good deal of initial failure and repetitious teaching as the teacher explains the same misunderstood process or concept over and over again to different children. It is far more economical of time and more likely to bring pupil success if children at a similar level of achievement are brought together for a proper explanation and discussion of the process.

Avoiding repetition

One of the challenges facing teachers of a mixed age/ability class is the two- to four-year age range among the pupils. Children may remain in the class for up to four years. Not for these teachers the luxury of the annually repeated project, the yearly exploration of the same familiar aspect of the environment or the repeated educational visit; not for them the teaching year by year of a group of concepts and skills restricted to a particular stage of children's academic or physical development.

It has been suggested that in these circumstances an appropriate mixture of small group and individual teaching will best meet the demands of subjects where very specific and graded skills and concepts are involved as in certain areas of language, maths and science. However, in the humanities, social and environmental studies, where a more general range of knowledge, learning skills and concepts can be involved, the more usual approach will be through a project or theme involving the whole class. It is an appropriate and popular approach. For the teacher of the mixed age/ability class certain problems have to be met and overcome:
- The teacher has to accept that projects have to be based on a two-, three- or four-year cycle, according to the number of age bands in the class, and plan the work with this in mind.
- The chronological pattern, sometimes followed in larger schools with single-year-group classes, when history-based topics move through history as the children move through the school, has

always been unsuitable for the small school. Topics which follow a specific theme through a broad band of time avoid the complexities of a strictly chronological approach in a class with a wide age range.
- The project planned has to meet the needs of varying levels of achievement and ability. The activities arranged and the materials, including work cards used, have to be sensitive to this fact and a great deal of time and care devoted to their creation.
- A closer and more detailed look at the planning of thematic project work in small schools is undertaken in chapter 3.

There is no escape from these simple facts of life in a mixed age/ability classroom. The successful teacher is likely to be one who has identified them and planned accordingly.

The small school and the under-5s

Primary schools have become increasingly involved with pre-school education and in chapter 6 we see how support is often given to the formation and sustaining of local playgroups and nursery classes.

Some schools have nursery classes attached to them as part of the same building, or sometimes in separate units on the school site. These units are more usual, however, in larger urban schools. In small schools the chances are that if the LEA has a policy of admitting rising-5s, perhaps at the start of the school year, then the infants teacher will be facing a class with an age range of just over 4 to just under 8 years. It is a daunting task. Many of the strategies for self-directed study which can be used with older infants and juniors are impossible with reception infants who need frequent attention. We shall see in the following pages how an imaginative organisation of the school day allows many teachers to cope with the challenge of this extended age range. It may be appropriate at this point, however, to list some of the ways in which the special needs of these very young children can be met:

- The classroom can be arranged, as described in the previous chapter, to allow for a variety of creative play and other activities.
- There should be a proper provision of suitable equipment and resources. There should be no admission of under-5s unless the LEA provides these.
- An infants-aid or classroom assistant should be employed.
- Parents and others can be drawn in as voluntary helpers. Many infants classes have willing help from active senior citizens.
- Team-teaching can allow for uninterrupted time with reception pupils when older infants are drawn off into other teachers' groups.

- Area discussion groups can be arranged, meeting in members' schools in turn.
- Support from specialist advisory and peripatetic staff should be arranged.
- In-service courses should be aimed at confronting these particular problems.

Opportunities in the mixed age/ability class

It would be quite wrong to leave this brief consideration of the characteristics of mixed age/ability classes without mention of some of the opportunities which such classes present, opportunities important enough to encourage a considerable number of large schools to arrange for children to spend two years with the same teacher in a class with two year-groups even though numbers allow for alternatives. Many of the advantages associated with classes of mixed age, are the same as those relating to small schools (see Introduction). They include the following:
- The special and productive relationship between teacher and pupil which a sustained contact can encourage.
- A deeper knowledge of the pupil's educational needs made possible for the teacher.
- The opportunity for ensuring continuity in the pupil's academic and personal growth.
- The encouragement of qualities of leadership, caring and responsibility afforded to the older pupils as they work with younger and less-developed children.
- The social development motivated by the mixing of children of different ages and developmental stages.

The alert teacher will make good use of these and any other advantages.

Summary

Arising from all the factors considered above, teachers of mixed age/ability classes may find it helpful to consider the following suggestions when organising their classes.
1 As always, it is very important to know what every activity undertaken by the children is meant to achieve; when it will take place and for how long; where it will take place and what suitable accommodation is available; what resources are needed and that they are provided; with whom – if anyone – the activity is shared.

2 Be flexible in the use of groupings. In these circumstances the small group formed for a particular purpose is often more helpful than a permanent grouping. Opportunities for whole class teaching may be more limited but do exist, can afford economies in time and should not be neglected.
3 Individual programmes of work for each pupil have value, but there are dangers to be aware of such as the excessive demand on a teacher's time as explanations are repeated; the very limited amount of time that can be given to any one child; the loss of stimulation and interaction found in group or class discussion; the danger of isolation within a busy classroom.
4 In organising the school day it is very important to keep in mind the differences between activities which are demanding of teacher attention and those that are less so. The difficulties which are caused by having all the children, at the same time, carrying out activities high in teacher demand are great.
5 There has to be an acceptance that the wide age range among the pupils in the class affects the cycle and presentation of thematic project work. Projects may not be repeatable for up to four years unless the presentation is greatly altered and the objectives ensure development and not unnecessary repetition. Following a chronological sequence in history-based projects is difficult and a broad-based project covering a wider span of time may be more suitable. Particularly careful planning and detailed preparation of all projects are called for as activities have to be arranged which meet a wide variety of abilities, ages and interests. (Project work is considered in detail in chapter 3.)
6 Being aware of the positive advantages as well as the difficulties presented by the mixed age/ability class is important. The opportunities offered by the sustained contact between pupil and teacher already outlined should be seized and the chance to foster qualities of leadership, care and responsibility among the older children taken.
7 The layout of the classroom must respond to the nature of the class and the activities which will take place. Too often teachers continue to layout classrooms where mixed-ability teaching is going to take place as if the class was a single-year-group. This has already been looked at in detail in chapter 1, but its importance needs to be stressed.

The use of other adults, including parents, in the mixed age/ability classroom and the value of co-operative teaching are considered later in this chapter.

Organising time: responses to the mixed age/ability class

Organising the school day and arranging the balance of activities for the week or term present a challenge to all teachers but for those in a small school faced with a class with very wide-ranging ages and abilities the problems presented are perhaps even greater. In the preceding pages the nature of these problems has been examined and some general principles suggested in dealing with the challenge they represent. We now apply these general principles to the actual classroom and suggest some possible patterns for the organisation of the school day.

Certain assumptions are made. The first of these is that the teacher has set out the classroom in ways not too dissimilar to the layouts suggested in chapter 1. The arrangement of the room must allow a variety of activities to take place at the same time, particularly group teaching alongside self-directed pupil activity. This is really very important and teachers are asked to consider the following suggestions for organising the school day alongside the layouts suggested in the previous chapter. The second assumption is that the teacher is willing to operate a flexible system of grouping and group teaching mixed with a certain amount of individual self-directed work and class discussion. If these two basic assumptions are met then the following suggestions for organising the day in a variety of mixed age/ability classes should be acceptable.

The organisations presented were drawn up on the basis of discussions held with involved teachers; long experience in small schools; and observation in hundreds of classrooms over many years. They are only suggestions and clearly leave room for much individual variation. The chapter concludes with detailed descriptions of actual classrooms in three small schools and includes a typical programme as operated in those schools. They are described with the knowledge that most teachers, even in large schools, have little opportunity to visit other classrooms, and such opportunity is even more restricted in small schools, which are often geographically isolated from others.

Simulated classroom models

The simulated classrooms described below are as follows:

Junior room: the junior class in a two-teacher school
There are 28 pupils in the class. The age-range covers the four junior years with children becoming 8 years of age in their first year and 11+ in their final year. The room is set out in a similar way to Figure 1 on page 4.

Teaching together: a two-teacher school
Two teachers have decided to work very closely together and to share responsibility for teaching all the children while retaining general pastoral responsibility either for the junior or for the infants group. The rooms are set out as in Figure 3 on page 8.

Teaching together: a two-teacher Junior co-operative unit in a three-teacher primary school
The unit is in a three-teacher school of 70 pupils. There are 48 pupils in the unit, all juniors except for three able and mature top infants. Teaching of all the children is shared but teachers retain separate pastoral responsibility for either upper or lower junior groups. Room layout is as Figure 4(c) on page 13.

The teachers in all these schools use help from other adults, mainly parents but also other members of the community with helpful skills.

Junior room

The junior class of 28 pupils is in a two-teacher school and has a four-year age range and a wide ability span. The classroom has been set out for mixed-ability teaching (see Figure 1 on page 4). The children's personal books are kept in trays in the tray bank. Each chair has a sturdy cloth satchel on its back to hold a pupil's books while he or she is using that particular work position. This avoids trays cluttering table and worktops.

The teacher uses a mixture of small group teaching, teacher-prescribed and self-directed individual pupil work, large group instruction where appropriate, and frequent, regular sessions of class discussion. Grouping is flexible but the children belong to a colour group (Blue, Red, Green, Yellow) for pastoral and some teaching purposes.

Children gather with the teacher in the group teaching base for instruction and discussion in small groups which are assembled for a particular goal. Children carrying out teacher-prescribed and self-directed activities, whether individually or in a group, use any work position suitable for that activity. For class discussion, television viewing or similar activities the children gather on the carpeted area surrounding the teacher base. For class teaching which needs a writing surface the children go to an assigned place at one of the desks, tables or carrels; these positions are retained for this purpose throughout the term.

The pattern of a typical day may be as follows. (The teacher uses the differential between teacher-demanding and self-directed activity extensively in organising the school day.)

9.00 Gathering time around the teacher base for morning worship, personal news and class discussion. Yesterday's activities reviewed, today's activities discussed. Grouping arranged for small group instruction; two groups, each of seven children, will be involved with this up to break time. The teacher ensures that the remaining 14 children are clear as to the self-directed activity they are to follow, and that they have the appropriate resources and work positions. The individual assignment/record books of the seven children in Red group are returned with comments and suggestions.

9.30 Teacher works with two maths groups. These groups are by achievement and not related to age. Teacher introduces or reinforces skills and concepts. One group is in the group teaching corner, the other around the nearby group work table. The remaining children are doing self-directed work. They choose their own timing but are expected to meet weekly targets designated in their personal record/assignment book. This self-directed activity can include the following:
(a) Personal interest projects. These may include written work, library research, practical investigation, etc. (A more detailed consideration of the nature and value of interest projects is made in chapter 3.)
(b) Completion of maths or language assignments arising from previous group teaching sessions. Queries are left to the next group session – the teacher is not interrupted at this point.
(c) Written or practical work, including science investigations or practical maths, arising from the current class thematic project.
(d) Library time. The children can spend some time reading in the library corner.

10.30 Break

10.45 Class session. Teacher introduces a language topic aimed at getting children to express opinions orally and in writing. The topic concerns zoos, their uses and limitations, and leads on to consideration of the worldwide conflict between humans and animals for living space. The topic is suitable for the whole class and allows for responses at the level of each child's own ability. Some of the written work will be suitable for completion in pupils' self-directed study time.

12.00 Lunch

1.30 Reading. Teacher works with slower readers; a parent supervises those who need help with an occasional word.

1.35 Gathering time. Children gather in the library corner. Teacher discusses some new books which have arrived and a new author. Children are encouraged to talk about the books they are currently reading. The teacher then introduces the afternoon's thematic project, reviews the work of the last project session and previews the activity for today. The class is involved in a project whose theme is 'Fire, Wind and Water'. The teacher checks that each group knows what they will be doing this afternoon. The groups are of mixed ability and age; children have been given some opportunity, within practical limits, to join the group which is of most interest to them.

1.50 Children collect in project groups and begin the various activities connected with it. (Some suggestions on the organisation of thematic projects with mixed age/ability classes are given in chapter 3.)

3.15 Gathering time. Children gather around the teacher base for review of the project and to listen to any points the teacher wishes to make. A story or discussion of some matter of interest to the class may follow. Before the children disperse the teacher collects the individual assignment/record books of the children in Blue group along with their interest projects and other work that needs attention.

3.35 Home time

A school day such as this, although straightforward and common enough in itself, includes features worthy of note because of their importance in organising successfully a class containing a wide range of age and ability. The most important of these features are the following:

(a) Although there is a wide range of ability and age in the class, the use of small group teaching, allied to well-organised self-directed activity by other pupils, allows for specific skills and concepts to be thoroughly taught to children of similar need with an economic use of teacher time. It allows for properly developed discussion among the children and fuller, uninterrupted exposition by the teacher.

(b) The 'gathering time' sessions hold the class together as an entity, which is important in many ways, not least in order to strengthen pupil/teacher relationships and to foster confidence and security among the children. It also allows the teacher to clarify for the children the purpose of the activities which are about to take place; this is of particular importance to children who – because of the

nature of the class – take more than the usual responsibility for directing their own studies.
(c) The self-directed activity is kept orderly and productive by the individual assignment/record books which allow the teacher to monitor the quantity and quality of work undertaken.
(d) The opportunity to teach with the whole class is taken in the language topic session which allows for common input but a varied level of response.

The weekly programme for the class will see a similar pattern to the above for four mornings, with each of the four maths groups having two group tutorial sessions. The period after morning break on four mornings is used either for a class language topic which allows for varied levels of response or for small group teaching of specific language skills on the pattern of the maths tutorials. Four afternoons are given to thematic projects which embrace work in history, geography, religious education, environmental studies and science. The actual activity flowing from the theme may embrace two- and three-dimensional art, craft, music, drama, library research, practical investigation and out-of-school visiting as well as written work which may be picked up in the morning language sessions. The remaining morning and afternoon periods are given to physical education and games.

Teaching together: a two-teacher primary school

This model depicts a two-teacher primary school with 44 pupils aged 5 to 11+. The headteacher is Mr J and the second teacher is Mrs M. There is a part-time teacher for two half-days a week. The classrooms have been set out in a way similar to that illustrated in Figure 3 on page 8.

The teachers follow a system of co-operative teaching. Although Mr J retains pastoral and registration responsibility for the juniors and Mrs M for the infants, the teaching programme is planned jointly. The teachers decided that by working very closely together they might better meet their pupils' needs. They defined the advantages of co-operative teaching and set out the following aims:
(a) Teachers will retain regular contact with all the children to help offset the lack of adult contacts for the pupils in this small school.
(b) Being aware that a small staff limits the range of special skills, training and interests, teachers have examined and recorded their own and will make themselves available to all age groups. A vigorous attempt will be made to close serious gaps in expertise through a planned programme of in-service training and peripatetic help.

(c) Teachers will seek through closer co-operation a more effective use of teacher time and material resources.
(d) Grouping will be kept flexible and will allow for movement between the age groups.
(e) There will be regular gatherings of the whole school to foster in the children a feeling of belonging to a secure and cohesive school 'family' of teachers and schoolmates.
(f) Older children will be given opportunities that will foster attitudes of leadership and responsibility.

The two teachers spend some time after school each day reviewing the day's activities and looking ahead to the next day. They also take the opportunity to discuss any particular pupil who may be giving concern. At times more significant developments for the school are discussed and plans made. All pupil records are kept centrally and are available readily to both teachers.

The pattern of work in both pastoral groups in general follows that described above for the junior room. However, significant differences arise from the decision of the teachers to work co-operatively. Thus a typical day may have the following structure:

9.00 The whole school gathers around the library and central teacher base for the morning assembly and the act of worship. Notices are given out and news shared.

9.15 Junior and infants pastoral groups separate and go to their own home base areas for briefing on the day's activities.

9.30 The juniors start either in maths groups with Mr J or on self-directed work. The maths groups include three older infants who are advanced in maths. The infants are busy with language activity, floor play and number work. Mrs M also has an eye on two slower-learning juniors who are using some of the simpler number apparatus. They refer to her if they need help. Two infants are working on a simple science experiment in the science bay; an older junior is helping them.

10.30 Break

10.45 Mrs M, who had holidays this year in Spain, is showing some holiday slides to the juniors and older infants. Later she will use holiday brochures to introduce some simple work on persuasive writing. Mr J is taking the opportunity to get to know the new arrivals and younger infants, making good use of his musical skills.

12.00 Lunch

1.15 Reading groups. Two parents join the teachers and supervise the more able readers. The teachers concentrate on the children needing most help.

1.40 The whole school gathers to be re-introduced to the thematic work the school is following. The topic is 'The Sea' and both teachers have been involved in planning this project and evolving activities which will be suitable for the various ages, interests and abilities of the children. They have used not only their special expertise as infant or junior phase teachers but also their specialist subject skills and interests. Thus while Mrs M has led in developing activities in the visual arts and language, Mr J has set up most of the science and environmental studies. They have shared their skills in music and drama to develop a simple musical play about the sea which will be worked up later as an end-of-term entertainment. One visit to a seaside town and its aquarium has already been made and other visits are planned. A retired local sea captain has been invited to visit the school.

3.15 The project work is cleared. Mr J wants a few moments with the 11+ leavers and Mrs M has the remaining younger juniors with her for a story.

3.35 Home time

It is not meant to suggest that this brief description of a school day is in any way a pattern for working a co-operative system of teaching in a two-teacher school. Such co-operation calls for considerable commitment by both teachers, some loss of classroom autonomy and a firm belief in the advantages that co-operation can bring; above all it calls for careful planning. What this sample day is meant to show is that it is possible to use space, resources, teachers' time and teachers' skills in ways that are different from those usually practised.

Among the gains which are illustrated are the following:
(a) The movement of the three infants to join the junior maths groups is encouraged by the open planning of the unit and the close liaison of the teachers. Flexible grouping across the classes is made easier.
(b) The use of the infants number apparatus by the juniors and the use of the shared science area by two infants illustrates the value of shared resources and facilities.
(c) The help given to the infants in the science area by the junior child demonstrates the opportunity offered under this system for encouraging responsible, helpful attitudes among the older children.
(d) The infants teacher uses her holiday experiences and special skills in language to benefit children outside her own pastoral group and this also presents an opportunity for the headteacher to work with the

youngest children. Such exchanges would be less likely without joint planning.
(e) There is easy access to the shared library which itself offers a wider selection of books simply because it is the shared book resource of two classes. The reading groups are also formed from a broader base.
(f) The jointly planned thematic project has allowed a sharing of ideas in its preparation, and during its implementation will continue to make the skills and interests of both teachers readily available to all the children. There will be a wider range of resources and activity bays available than would be likely in a more traditional, separate-class organisation. The pupil grouping, whether for common interest or common goal, is again made on a broader base.
(g) The final session illustrates how co-operation can allow a period of uninterrupted withdrawal by a teacher with a small selected group.

The rest of the week would be very likely to bring more examples of the opportunities created by co-operative teaching in a two-teacher school.

Teaching together: a two-teacher junior co-operative unit in a three-teacher primary school

In this simulated school of 70 pupils the two junior teachers have formed a co-operative or teamed unit for the 46 junior children. They have partially opened the screen which separates their rooms and laid out the combined space in a way similar to that of Figure 4(c) on page 13. One room has been arranged as a quiet room containing the library corner, the microcomputer base and a large number of positions suitable for quiet, individual study. The quiet room can also be used for class teaching. The second room contains work surfaces and bays for more practical activities. Part of the room is screened by tall cupboards as a group teaching area.

Because the children are all juniors and more homogeneous in age and ability than the children in the infants/junior unit previously described, the teachers do not identify with upper or lower age groups as often and their teaching is more integrated. For the purposes of liaison with parents and registration, however, they each have a pastoral group. This does not have to relate to pupils' ages but it is simpler and more convenient if it does. Other than that the two teachers share responsibility for the education of all the children.

The teachers, having defined the advantages that will be gained from very close co-operation, have decided to organise the school day

and approach the various aspects of the curriculum in the following ways:
(a) The children will gather together frequently with both teachers.
(b) Grouping will be flexible and reflect the needs of the pupils at that point in their development. Age will be only one criterion in many when forming groups.
(c) Teacher skills and interests will be used to the benefit of all the children.
(d) All resources and facilities will be shared and available as appropriate to all the children.
(e) Planning the curriculum will be a joint process and its implementation will involve a close integration of the two teachers' activities.
(f) Evaluation of pupils' progress and evaluation of the curriculum will also be a joint process involving both teachers:

Mathematics The children are divided initially into eight groups broadly reflecting their stage of development in this subject. Each teacher has charge of four groups. On Monday and Wednesday teacher A is free to withdraw with any of his/her maths groups to the group teaching area. Teacher B will supervise the remaining children, who will be doing self-directed work, plus the remainder of A's maths groups carrying out maths work prescribed by A. On Tuesdays and Thursdays the situation is reversed with teacher B being free to withdraw groups.

Language A good deal of the language development is drawn from oral and written work across the curriculum. When a particular technical skill such as punctuation, construction, handwriting or spelling has to be more specifically taught, a temporary group is formed of those who need this instruction and it is given in the group teaching area by one of the teachers. A more broadly-based language topic – for instance an introduction to different kinds of writing, such as writing to persuade, to present an argument, to record or report – is more likely to be taken with a class-sized group.

Humanities and science These and other aspects of the curriculum such as art and drama are normally contained within the thematic project approach used by the unit. Where these are taught as separate subjects there is some specialisation by the teachers. Projects are planned and implemented jointly by both teachers, each leading in her/his skill areas.

Reading There is one shared library offering easy access and a wider selection of books than is possible with a single class. One teacher has responsibility for improving the performance of less able readers while the other supervises the library and fosters interest by discussion and display.

Physical education and games Teachers specialise in the areas in which they have most skill. Games choice for the children is maximised.

A day in this two-teacher unit could take the following form.

9.00 The children of the unit assemble with their two teachers together in the quiet room. Morning worship and school news are given and then the children are briefed on the activities for the day.

9.30 Teacher A takes two maths groups – about a dozen pupils in all – to the group teaching area. Each group will contain children at a similar point in their development in mathematics. The teacher works with each group on new concepts and skills, reinforces what is already held and discusses work done in self-directed periods. Before the session ends the teacher provides follow-up work for the next self-directed period and ensures that there is a good understanding of the concepts involved and a reasonable chance of success.

Teacher B has charge of the remaining children. These are involved in self-directed activity. This includes follow-up work from their own tutorial periods in maths and language. They may also be involved with personal interest projects or activity connected to the thematic project that the whole unit is undertaking. The nature of their activity may involve writing at one of the positions in the quiet room; book research in the library area; experimentation in the science or maths bays; two- or three-dimensional art linked to their projects; problem-solving with the microcomputer, using prepared programmes. They may be working singly, in pairs or in very small groups. Although the work has been discussed in the group tutorials or project time and involves well-understood or carefully structured materials aimed at independent study, the child may need guidance from time to time and will receive that from teacher B, who in this role sustains and supports rather than initiates new activity.

10.30 Break

10.45 Teacher B withdraws with 12 children to the group tutorial area. They are older children, many of whom will be going up to the secondary school shortly. The teacher has been doing a short series of lessons with them on recording and taking notes.

Teacher A has the remaining children. They have been involved with a topic concerned with description and the use of this when writing stories. Today they are describing times which are special to them. The topic allows for a response at different levels of age and ability.

12.00   Lunch

1.15   The whole unit is involved with a class thematic project. The title is 'Caring World'. It has involved the children in geographical, historical and social studies. Science, art, music and drama have all been included as the children have found out about Third World countries, patterns of care in the past, made some tests on soil and examined the effects of drought, studied the music, art and dance of Africa and India – and much else. (A more detailed development of this type of project may be found in chapter 3.)

The two teachers, with some assistance from the part-time teacher, have planned this topic together. They have involved one parent on a regular basis and brought in other people from the community who have particular associations with caring agencies or who have visited the Third World. The session this afternoon will end with a visit by the local agent from OXFAM to talk about the work of the organisation. The children have a 10-minute break during the afternoon.

3.00   The topic work is cleared and the children settle to a quiet period of reading. The teachers work with those in need.

3.25   The whole unit gathers for comment on the day's activities.

3.30   Home time

It is not suggested that this pattern for a school day in a two-teacher co-operative unit is the only one. The greater variety of space and the wider range of resources than are likely in one classroom, in addition to the more flexible use of time that comes with close co-operation, make possible a variety of patterns for the school day. During the course of the week the unit may see teachers making use of their specific skills in physical education, in religious studies or in further periods of art, drama or music. They may at times be teaching quite separately, have large or small groups, be tutoring or supervising.

What is certain about the week in such a unit is that it will offer the teachers opportunity for professional dialogue and a chance to plan and implement educational activity for the children in partnership. There will be a broadened opportunity to use their special skills, interests and training. Assessments of pupil progress and curriculum will benefit from the knowledge and experience of both teachers being brought to the discussion. If behavioural or emotional problems arise with a pupil, a broader perspective will be available in seeking solutions.

For the children the larger number of pupils in the unit provides a greater flexibility in grouping, increases the opportunity to share an activity with someone of similar interest or achievement and widens the range of social contact. There is access both academically and pastorally to more than one adult and to a wide range of resources and facilities.

Note
The three models examined above – the junior room, the two-teacher school and the two-teacher junior unit – have been created to illustrate different approaches to the organisation of the school day when teachers are faced with classes of wide ability and age span. However, work which closely echoes these approaches is to be found in many schools in various parts of Britain. There follow examples of actual current practice observed in three schools by the author.

Examples of current practice
Primary school with junior co-operative unit

There are four classes and approximately 100 pupils. The school is on two sites separated by a lane. The infants are housed in the old school building and the 50 juniors in a newer block which also includes the staff and office accommodation. The school has been waiting since the 1960s for the completion of this block in order that the infants can join the juniors on the same school site. All the junior children are taught in an open co-operative unit which provides an excellent working example of the co-operative teaching described in the previous pages. There are plans for the infants to move towards the same co-operative teaching organisation.

The junior co-operative unit

The 50 junior children are taught by the headteacher and the junior teacher, with assistance from a part-time teacher, in a co-operative unit of linked rooms. These were originally separated rooms but an archway has been made in the joining wall to form an open unit with appropriate activity and resource bays. The plan of the unit (Figure 7) and the photograph (Figure 8) illustrate more clearly how the rooms are laid out. The bays are around the perimeter of the rooms. Included in the unit are the following resource and activity areas:
– Two adjoining practical bays, well-equipped with easily-accessible resources and including a cooker. There are large work surfaces.
– Two computer positions.
– Two library bays – fiction and reference – with comfortable seating.
– A reading help corner with word-building and other aids.
– A central spine of tables linking the two rooms and providing general work positions.

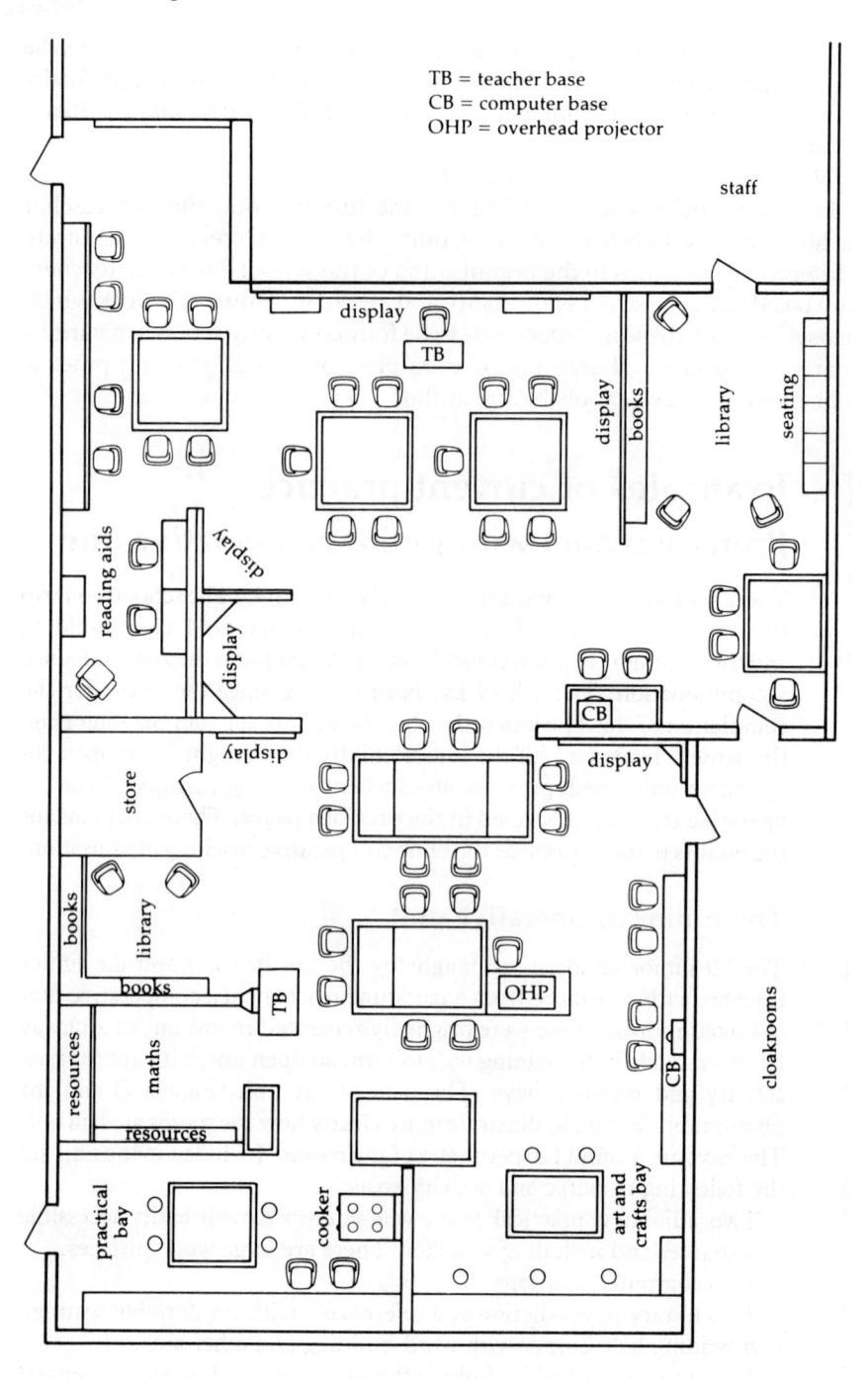

7. Co-operative unit: two teachers, 50 pupils.

8. A primary school co-operative junior unit.

- Maths and science bay.
- A large walk-in store.

Organisation

The teachers retain pastoral care of either upper or lower juniors and each group has a general home base in one of the two rooms. However, the programme of activities for the children is decided, planned, implemented and evaluated by the two teachers jointly and there is an integrated use of resources, space and facilities.

There is a considerable amount of joint planning over the longer term by the whole staff, including the infants teachers, to decide on the general themes upon which the bulk of the children's work is centred. However, the more detailed day-to-day planning is carried out for the unit by the two teachers involved (the head and a junior teacher) who meet each day before school to discuss and plan the day's activities in line with longer-term objectives already decided.

The organisation of the unit's activity is best illustrated by outlining a typical school day within it.

8.30   The staff meet to discuss the day's activities. There is an attempt to bring some fresh and stimulating input to each day.

8.40   The children are allowed into the classroom to use the computers, read or do other quiet activity.

9.00   The children go to their pastoral groups for registration.

9.10   The headteacher takes a group of children for a drama session. The theme this half-term is 'The Romans' and the drama relates to this. The junior teacher is doing maths and computer work assisted by the part-time teacher. The computer work is related to the Roman theme and involves problem-solving.

10.00 The headteacher returns from drama. The part-time teacher begins a language session with a group of children who are writing articles, news stories and other items for a mock Roman newspaper. The junior teacher continues with another group on computers and maths, and the headteacher joins him.

10.40 Break

11.00 The part-time teacher tells the whole unit the story of Pompeii, its destruction and excavation. The headteacher sees a visitor and the junior teacher prepares some materials.

11.30 One of the day's set sessions: all the children in the unit go to reading groups.

12.00 Lunch

1.00 Registration in pastoral groups, then the whole unit gathers for a briefing on the afternoon's activities.

1.15 Project work. The unit is engaged in two- and three-dimensional art, music, expressive writing and computer studies, connected for the most part with the Roman project.
In line with the school's policy of involving other adults in the classroom, the three teachers are joined by two other people. The supervision of pupil activity is as follows:
The headteacher has a group printing from polystyrene pattern cuts.
The secretary/classroom assistant (the LEA allows this very useful joint-role appointment) has a group making a large Roman-style mosaic pattern.
The part-time teacher is adding illustrations and more writing to the Roman newspaper with another group.
A secondary school music teacher has a regular session with a recorder group.
The junior teacher is working with a computer group on an Arrow programme (a popular computer program for primary schools).

2.30 As this is Friday the whole school assembles in the small hall for discussion of the week's activities in each class. The process is unhurried and involves many children, infant and junior.

3.15 Home time

Fixed points during the school week include the following:
Tuesday Music teaching is reinforced by the visits of a music student as well as the visits of the secondary school music teacher
Wednesday Team and small group games
Thursday Swimming at 9.30

Curriculum: points of special interest

General approach A topic or thematic approach is followed which covers much of the basic skill work as well as more exploratory areas of the curriculum. A detailed flow chart or study web is prepared for the start of each term indicating areas of study and how these may be developed. The web is extended and given more detail as the topic progresses. A careful balance is kept between the amount of time spent, within the topic, on the study of language, humanities, maths, science and the creative arts.

Language This is often but not solely related to the thematic work. A range of writing purposes are covered, discussion is encouraged and the mastery of technical skills is related to the improvement of the expressive and recording work undertaken.

Maths Again this is often drawn from the thematic work (wages bills from a Roman museum, for example) but with reference to listed skills and concepts which the school aims to cover.

Humanities History, geography and religious studies are integrated into the current theme.

Science This is integrated within the current theme.

Computer studies The two computers are largely used as tools for problem-solving within the current topic. The junior teacher gives considerable time to helping pupils master the technical skills necessary.

Creative arts Creative work emerges mainly from the thematic work. Recently a joint undertaking with other schools, including the local secondary school, chose Indian music, art, dance, drama and poetry as a theme. There were visits from Indian dancers and musicians, and an exhibition of Indian artistic and other products.

Visits and educational excursions There is a strong emphasis on first-hand experience. A minibus is shared with three other schools. Educational field trips, some residential, are frequent.

Comment

This junior unit illustrates many of the advantages which are claimed for co-operative teaching:
- The use of teachers' special skills is facilitated, e.g. the junior teacher's skill in computer work, the head's interest in drama.
- All the junior children have access during the day to the skills and interests of all three teachers.
- There is greater flexibility and choice in the formation of groups for particular purposes, e.g. the range of activity groups formed on the afternoon of the day illustrated.
- For the headteacher in particular, being called from the room does not mean leaving an unsupervised class.
- The resources of both classes are more easily accessible to all the pupils in the unit and are more varied.
- The larger amount of space available allows for greater variety of provision, e.g. the variety of work stations, resource and activity bays provided in the unit.
- The stimulation and support gained from the joint planning and implementation of projects was commented on by staff.

The school is deeply involved with the community and draws in a considerable number of parents and other adults to help both inside and outside the classrooms. The size and open nature of the junior unit facilitates this process. The success of the junior unit has encouraged preliminary moves by the infants classes to follow suit.

★

Primary school with infants co-operative unit

The original building of this four-teacher school – two infants and two junior classes – is now used as the school hall and a new four-class unit with staff accommodation has been added nearby. The two infants classrooms were divided by a screen but this is never closed. A team-teaching system is used for all the infants in what is now an attractive open-plan area.

The infants co-operative unit

There are 46 children in the unit, aged from rising 5 to 7+. There are two teachers and a classroom assistant who is present each morning and one afternoon during the week.

The unit layout

The unit is formed from two average-sized classrooms originally separated by a screen which is now permanently drawn back. The unit is set out to provide a series of areas which relate to particular categories of activities. There are areas designated as follows:
– a maths area
– a language area
– an art and craft area
– a role-play area
– a writing area
– two home bases.

The different areas are separated from each other by display units, cupboards and bookcases but these do not obstruct free movement from one area to another and are low enough for teachers to have a good view of the unit from almost any position. Resources are adequate and very accessible. Some carpeting and soft flooring reduces noise from movement of chairs and equipment. The plan in Figure 9 gives an indication of the position and relative size of each area, and Figure 10 shows the children at work in the unit.

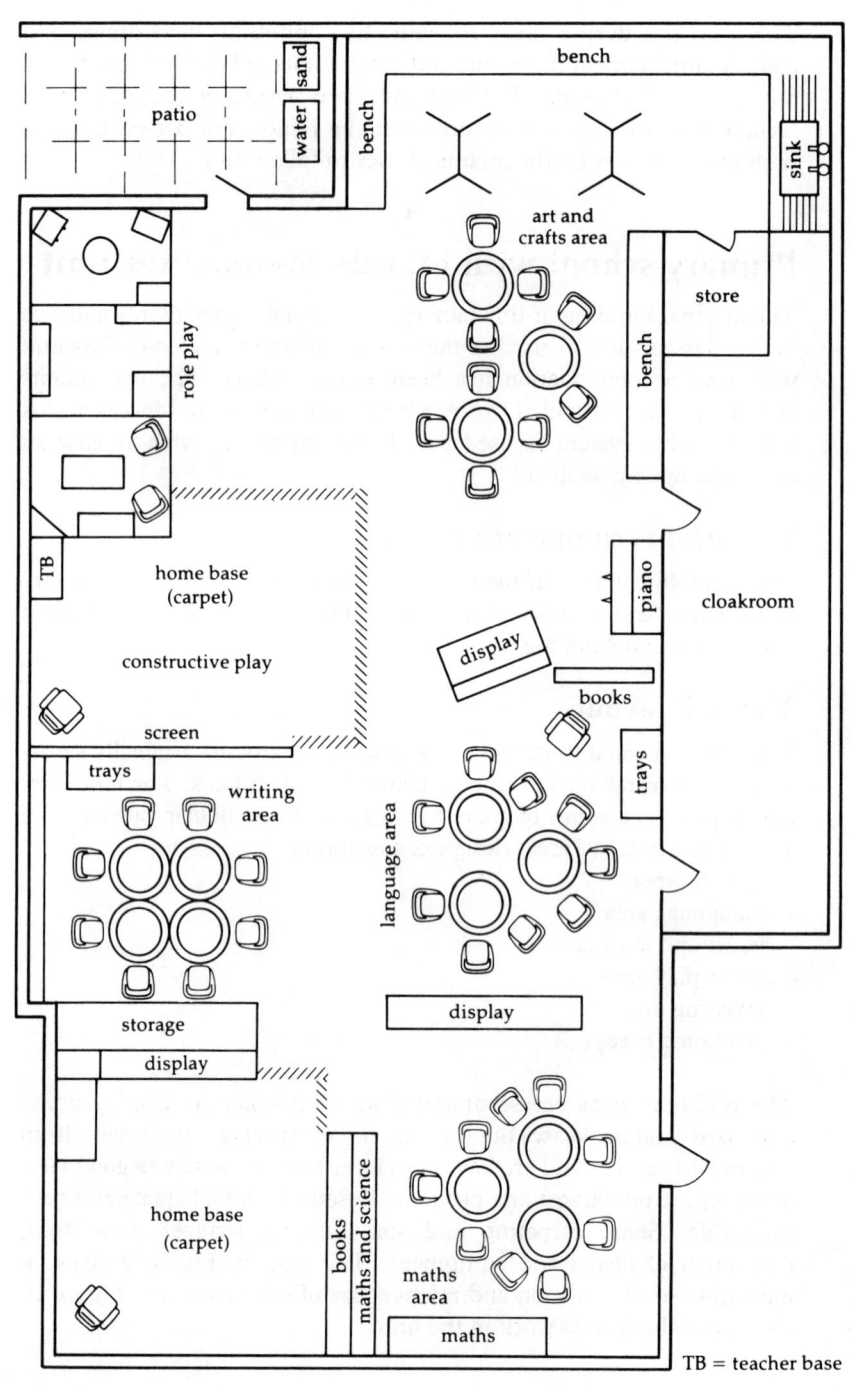

9. Infants co-operative unit: two teachers and a part-time classroom assistant, 46 pupils.

Organisation

The organisation is one sometimes referred to as a 'carousel' system. The children are organised in groups and move in turn to prepared activity areas.

In this unit there are five colour groups, each composed of about nine children. The groups are formed by reference to reading ability but other factors such as age are also considered. Every group goes to each one of the five designated activity areas during the course of the day. The pattern is the same each day for a week. As some set activity periods are missed on days when the class has physical education, singing or games, the unit works to a five-week cycle and each Monday the order in which groups go to specific activities alters. This avoids the same group missing a particular activity each week. The place where each group is and the activities the children are to follow are clearly and colourfully illustrated and children appear to have no difficulty in knowing where they should be and what they should be doing.

The children are also arranged in two pastoral groups, one made up of the older children and the other of the younger pupils. These groups are used for stories, physical education, games, news and on other occasions when a larger group is seen as advantageous. The whole unit gathers together for assemblies and music making.

The teachers each have charge of certain activity areas, one being responsible for maths and expressive writing, the other for language, creative or role-play activities and art/craft. The classroom assistant

10. Infants co-operative unit in action.

helps where necessary but concentrates mainly on children in the art and play areas. After two weeks the teachers change over responsibilities so that neither becomes identified with a particular subject.

Reading is taken after the midday break each day for 15 minutes. Physical education and games are taken at fixed times each week. Each teacher takes her own pastoral group for these activities. There are also periods spent with the teachers in pastoral groups in the home base areas.

The school day

9.00   Pastoral groups, register, news (or unit assembly)

9.35   Colour groups, Session One:
        Orange – maths
        Red   – language
        Blue   – writing
        Green – art
        Yellow – play

10.20   Break

10.45   Colour groups, Session Two:
        Yellow – maths
        Orange – language
        Red   – writing
        Blue   – art
        Green – play or hall time

11.15   Colour groups, Session Three:
        Green – maths
        Yellow – language
        Orange – writing
        Red   – art
        Blue   – play

12.00   Lunch

1.15   Pastoral groups: Library reading

1.30   Colour groups, Session Four:
        Blue   – maths
        Green – language
        Yellow – writing
        Orange – art
        Red   – play

2.10   Colour groups, Session Five:

Red — maths
Blue — language
Green — writing
Yellow — art
Orange — play

2.50 Clear up

3.00 Pastoral groups: story, discussion

3.15 Home time

Curriculum: points of special interest

Reading Each teacher aims to hear four children read when they pass through their area of responsibility.

The unit has use of the hall between 10.45 and 11.15 each day. The pastoral groups take alternate days to use it for physical education, music and large group activity in two weekly sessions. Other times of access to the hall can be arranged.

Writing The writing sessions are for expressive writing and handwriting skills. The language sessions deal with more structural language work.

Recording There is a standard reading record kept with the child and marked up by each teacher as the pupil is heard reading. Maths records are held in the maths area. Language schemes are graded and children's progress is recorded as they work through them.

Comment

The shared rooms allow for large activity areas which are well spaced and carry a greater variety of resources. The presence of two other adults for the majority of the week and the diversity of activity which allows some of the children to follow self-directed work, makes it possible to arrange uninterrupted teaching time with very small groups. The teachers benefit from the stimulation and mutual support gained from planning and implementing the education of the children together. They claim an observable improvement in behaviour and attitudes to work since the introduction of the co-operative organisation. The teachers use their special interests and skills to lead in work preparation and planning but do not to specialise in their teaching.

The carousel system is sometimes criticised for allowing the day to be fragmented, the activities to be unrelated and the children perhaps having to break off an activity at a productive point to change areas. These criticisms are countered in this unit by relating much of the work, including maths and language, to a central project theme which will run for some weeks. To avoid interruption at a crucial moment, children are allowed to stay on in an activity area if their work demands it.

Primary school: the infants room

This is a three-class school with a weighting towards the younger children. The infants class described has 26 pupils aged from rising 5 to 7 years of age – the full infants school range. The class is housed in a room of reasonable size which stands by itself away from the main school building.

The infants room layout

The room contains the following activity areas:
– A carpeted home base which is also used for floor play with constructional toys.
– An area for role play with suitable furnishings and equipment.
– A maths and science resource area.
– An art and craft area with bench and sink.
– A general work area with tables for individual or group activity.

In addition, part of an adjoining cloakroom has been arranged for water and sand play. There are wall boards for display and tables for collections and three-dimensional art and craft.

When the weather permits the yard outside is used for many activities that require more space. There is a village hall nearby which can be used by the school. Figure 11 illustrates the room layout in greater detail.

Organisation

The organisation is a mixture of small group teaching, teacher-prescribed individual pupil work, free choice activity and frequent whole class gatherings for discussion or instruction where appropriate.

Essentially there is recognition that the range of age and ability within the class makes it necessary to organise individual work or small group instruction – or a mixture of both. When children are working independently or in a self-directed way they may be working to targets set by the teacher or on an activity of their choice. In either case the order and timing of these activities is a matter for the pupil as long as prescribed work is completed within agreed time limits.

Much of the work, whether done in groups (there are five of these arranged by age) or individually, is likely to be set within a project theme which the whole class is exploring at that time. This provides a welcome link across the subject and activity boundaries, it can be the centre of class discussion, and it helps motivate and give cohesion to the class.

Teaching mixed age and ability classes 51

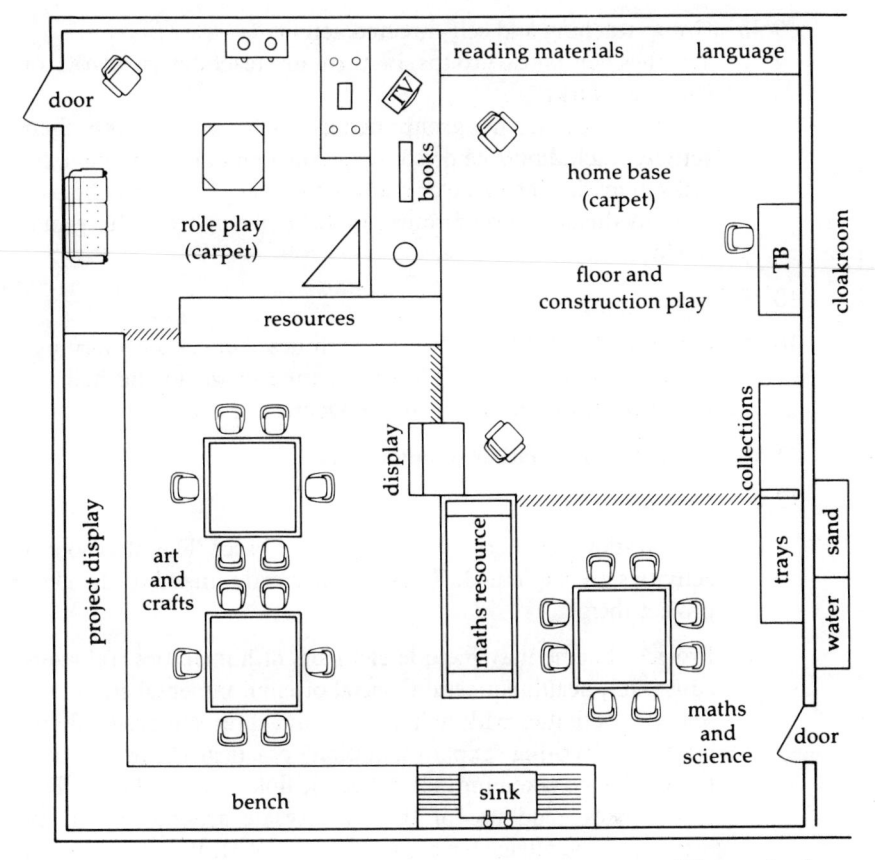

TB = teacher base

11. A primary school infants classroom.

The classroom is set out to allow the children following self-directed activity, whether individually or with companions, to work with minimum interference. Group teaching is usually in the home base or around one of the group tables. When the teacher is addressing the whole class or discussing something with them, the home base is the most likely venue.

The school day

The children are allowed access to the room before school starts and can use the play materials.

9.00 Registration. School or infants assembly. Discussion with the whole class in the home base. Children, especially the reception children, are encouraged to bring objects from home to talk about.

9.30 Group teaching and self-directed activity.
The teacher takes groups in turn for teaching in maths or language work.
Children not in the group being taught may choose their activity, including role or constructional play, but will have set tasks in maths, language or reading to cover. These may be part of individualised programmes or have arisen from the group session.

10.30 Break

10.45 Group and self-directed work continues. On certain mornings the class may watch a TV programme or go to the hall for physical education, music and movement or drama.

11.50 Clear-up time. Gather in home base.

12.00 Lunch

1.15 Registration. Gathering time in home base. The afternoon's activities are explained. These are normally linked to the class project theme.

1.30 Project. Theme may include elements of humanities, religious education, health education, social or environmental studies or science. Activities will include two- and three-dimensional art, craftwork, writing, experimentation, practical maths. Opportunity may be taken for making music linked to the theme. The class makes good use of the countryside around and many features of the village have also been explored. Parents help and some use is made of local people with special skills.

2.30 Break

2.45 Clear-up time. Change home books.
Home base for discussion, stories, songs, poems and drama.

3.15 Home time

Comment

This pattern of organising children's learning into periods of being directly taught in small groups, spending some time in activities which are more self-directed and allowing some freedom of choice and timing, is common to many infants rooms in small schools where the range of ability and age is wide. It calls for a number of preparatory and ongoing actions by the teacher:

(a) The room has to be set out to allow for both self-directed individual activity, group teaching and activity involving the whole class.

(b) Activity areas have to be well resourced and these resources kept easily available to young children who have to exercise responsibility for some of their own learning early in their school life. They have to learn quickly the importance of keeping the room in order and play their part in doing it.
(c) There has to be careful preparation of work for each group and the problem of ensuring continuity and proper matching is considerable.
(d) The teacher-prescribed activities carried out by the children in their self-directed periods have to respond to each pupil's needs if they are not to become a time-filling irrelevance. It calls for much preparation and recording away from the classroom.
(e) The range of age and ability means that the teacher has continually to switch mentally to meet educational needs that may be many years of development apart.

If operated successfully the system can not only give to children the proper literacy and other skills and knowledge they need but also develop self-reliant attitudes and an ability to organise their own work, make choices and adjust to different situations. They are qualities which have been commented on as being noticeable among pupils in small schools. However, the pressures upon the teacher are self-evident and both skill and dedication are demanded. It is fortunate that, as in the example above, so many small schools enjoy the services of such teachers. The possible harm done by a weaker teacher failing to cope with such pressure is related to the length of time pupils spend in such classrooms.

A final comment

I have been a believer in co-operative and team teaching for many years and long ago worked for a Schoolmaster Fellowship at Exeter, which culminated in a small book on the subject called 'Teaching Together'. It makes total sense to me to share expertise, time, space and resources. The gains I have set out fairly comprehensively in the preceding pages are real and obtainable. However, it would be quite unfair to leave the impression that there are no mountains to be climbed before the sunny uplands are discovered, no hidden crevice or lurking danger on the way.

The first and most obvious obstacle is that not all teachers admire each other enough to give up some of their classroom autonomy in pursuit of new goals. It is important that teachers who work closely together have regard and respect for each other. Generally any gap can be closed by a greater understanding of each other's methods. It helps to have clear objectives, and agreed policies worked out as to how these are to be reached. Discussion, time, explanation and example can work wonders but sometimes it is pointless to continue trying to put Genghis Khan with Little Red Riding Hood; the divide is just too great.

There are problems also in the sharing of resources harvested from tiny general allowances over many seasons. To have less than total control over the children who will use them is just too much for some colleagues. Usually the compensation of laying hands on someone else's resources is more than enough reward but not if the chap next door is education's Mr Micawber with barely a pencil to his name.

There are some complexities in arranging groups, recording progress and timetabling the use of shared resources which have to be worked through. There has also to be a system for settling professional disagreements which can, if not dealt with quickly, degenerate into more personal estrangements. But much is possible, given the will to succeed and a belief in the value of what is being attempted. It is a clear view of what is to be gained that can do most to foster success.

3 Curriculum opportunities

The general advantages and disadvantages offered by smaller schools have already been considered at some length (see introduction). Ways in which the effective use of space and the organisation of time can help to maximise these advantages and minimise the disadvantages have also been considered (chapter 2). But there are also within the curriculum itself particular areas of study which carry special opportunities or problems for small schools. The special problems for small schools within certain subject areas, such as maths and language, relate mainly to staffing, resources and organisation of a class with a wide spread of age and ability. These have already been examined. However, there are areas of study offering special opportunities which are affected by the size of the school and its location: environmental studies and social studies.

The HMI Primary Survey of 1979 ('Primary Education in England; A Survey by HM Inspectors', HMSO), points out the good use made of the environment by small schools and this may be partly due to the location of many small schools in the heart of the country. Surrounded by an environment that is rich in educational potential and in most cases safely accessible, it is perhaps not surprising that the report found such evidence. However, small urban schools may also be surrounded by exciting and rich environments – full of colour and vitality and waiting to be explored. This chapter looks at some of the ways in which the environment is used by small schools and makes some suggestions as to how the nature of this activity can be viewed and perhaps extended.

The second area of curriculum opportunity relates to the community that surrounds the school. Quite often that community is cohesive, has strongly-developed social structures, familiar landmarks, traditions, events and established leadership. Many schools have linked themselves closely to their communities and from these links have built a programme of social studies which is based in reality and is rich in first-hand experience.

Some comments on the aims of primary education are made, and the use of a project-type approach in social and environmental studies is examined through three simulated projects.

Curricular aims

The children at present in our primary schools will not reach adulthood until the 21st century. It would not be unreasonable to assume that those designing a primary school curriculum would, as a starting point, make some study of the likely demands of living in that century. Not to do so would risk developing skills, fostering attitudes and encouraging the acquisition of knowledge that will not be relevant to the needs of an individual living in the 21st century. However, such a study is not often undertaken and too rarely forms the starting point for discussion among teachers and others designing a curriculum. More often the new curriculum emerges from modifications to existing practice which has itself grown from a response to a past society which no longer exists.

The weight of traditional curriculum content tends to inhibit a realistic assessment of the probable future adult needs of our pupils and the designing of an appropriate curriculum around them. This is not to suggest that teachers and others involved do not consider the future needs of their children; clearly they do. What is suggested is that too little time is given to a thorough discussion of these before curriculum change and development is undertaken.

It is obviously not possible to predict precisely the demands of a future society but it does seem absurd to set out to prepare children for it without some view as to its nature. Such debate is outside the scope of this book but it is possible in examining the special curriculum opportunities offered by small schools to relate them to the more likely demands of that future society.

A persuasive society

Children growing up in our schools today will have to cope with a society which may well become ever more persuasive and manipulative because of the increasingly vivid and immediate impact of modern methods of communication. The movement towards a less authoritarian society and an increase in personal freedom and choice may well be obstructed by the use of new methods of communication to manipulate and deceive. In such a society it will become ever more important for individuals to be able not only to inform themselves but to validate that information, interpret it and use it to make choices and decisions. The ability to think critically and act independently has always been important but in a more complex society, where options are wider and the power of others to influence decisions by persuasion greater, then this capacity for independent thought increases in importance.

Technology

It is reasonable also to assume that the progress in technology which is making such an impact on our lives today will continue into the next century. Technology brings change and coping with change calls not only for some understanding of the technology involved but also the nature of the changes in society that it brings about. It is one thing to make every primary school child familiar with the microcomputer and how to work it – it is quite a different challenge to help those children understand the way such technology will affect the pattern of their working lives.

If technology can sustain production of our needs with far less labour then the likely effect must be longer periods of time when individuals are not engaged in production. If the fulfilment and sense of worth which comes from employment is threatened at some time then these have to be sought in other ways. Creative leisure pursuits may provide some of the answers but the satisfaction that can come through serving the community in voluntary ways may be far more fulfilling. It may be as important for children to know about the work of a Samaritan or a Marriage Guidance Counsellor as it is for them to know about the work of a miner, farmer, doctor or engineer. To fill the gaps in continuous employment that technology is already creating and to provide the satisfaction that a less fulfilling job may fail to give, then full involvement in the caring activity of a voluntary body may offer a solution.

To cope with the challenge of rapid change the individual needs to be prepared for it. There is a need to be secure and at ease in relationships with people of different ages and backgrounds, to be able to cope with changing patterns of work, to be knowledgeable in relevant ways and once again to be independent enough of mind to make choices and decisions based on validated information.

A threatened environment

One of the great challenges that has to be addressed today is the threat to the balanced ecology of our planet by the rapidly increasing human population. The demands this expanded population makes upon food production and the consumption of raw materials has resulted in the extensive destruction of natural habitats such as woodland, marsh and tropical forest. The result of rapid industrial growth has been the pollution of seas, land and air by waste products. The effect on Earth's wild animal population seems destined to become catastrophic.

All this is well known but the interdependence of humanity and the environment appears to be a lesson we are reluctant to learn; the destruction continues and must eventually seriously threaten the quality of our lives if not our very existence. The understanding of this threat should be a major item in any school curriculum. Such studies should lead not only to up-to-date knowledge but also to a grasp of the action which must be taken to combat this destruction. There is every reason to believe that when our present-day primary school children are adults the problem will be far from solved and it is surely of major importance that we prepare them to meet this particular challenge.

In practical terms this means devising a curriculum which looks forward to future needs, which uses some understanding of the past to probe and understand the challenges of the future and how to meet them. It means that concepts of cause and effect, continuity and change, stewardship and interdependence must be thoroughly understood and related to the real world. That real world starts outside the schoolroom door and it is into that world that our children have to be led. At the heart of the historical, geographical and scientific dimensions of social and environmental studies must lie an attempt to understand the urgency of this threat to humankind's existence and what has to be done to meet it. This is where all our history has led us; this alters our view of geography, ecology and the purposes of our environmental science in unprecedented ways. If we do not give our children these understandings then we shall not have prepared them adequately for their adult life and will have failed them in a fundamental way.

These are only three of the likely characteristics of the 21st century which are not too difficult to predict. There are others – all that is suggested here is that in considering the curriculum there are new dimensions which have to be taken into account and which relate to the nature of the society our children will occupy as adults. Much of the curriculum both in aim and content will be traditional and familiar.

Some comment on the knowledge, skills and personal qualities that are demanded by a curriculum which takes into account such dimensions as coping with a persuasive society, rapid change and environmental threat may be helpful at this point. This can then be related to the nature of the small school.

Knowledge, skills and personal qualities

The end-purpose of education must be to enable the individual to live a fulfilled life and to contribute something to the well-being of others. The achievement of this goal will depend very largely on that individual's ability to make wise choices and decisions at various points in life. To enable anyone to make balanced choices and to make and implement sensible decisions, that person needs to have certain attributes and a good curriculum is aimed at developing these. What are they? The following are suggested:

Being knowledgeable in relevant ways

It could be said that too much of our primary curriculum is concerned with the absorbing of facts which are not remembered and have little relevance to the present or future needs of the pupils. This is a criticism made with some justification. It may be timely, if we are concerned with a curriculum aimed at meeting future challenge as well as present necessity. It would be a dull curriculum indeed that only included strictly practical information and paid no attention to the cultural, aesthetic or spiritual dimensions, but there is factual content which has no real relevance which could be dispensed with and replaced.

Knowledge which relates to an understanding of the nature of present-day society, of the threat to the environment and of the effects of technology upon people's lives are examples of the sorts of knowledge that have become increasingly important.

Locating and validating knowledge

The retention of knowledge, of facts, by any individual is limited; thus the ability to locate and validate information when we need to is important. If we do not have that ability then we can be handicapped when we have to select options, make choices or voice opinions. Whether the information is to be found in print, by careful observation or by questioning these are skills that have to be developed by practice and the sooner children start the sooner they will become competent in them.

Discovery or investigative learning has been a feature of primary schools for many years although it is perhaps not quite so developed as is often claimed. What passes as discovery is at times no more than the slavish copying of passages of poorly understood information from textbooks. Much will depend on the nature and presentation of this task by teachers. Investigative learning is encouraged by the GCSE and other exams and this is having profound effects on the styles of teaching and learning in secondary schools. If it leads to a genuine ability to unearth information then it must be a welcome new emphasis.

Locating the information is of course only the beginning; it has to be validated, proved to be accurate and not accepted at face value. One of the more disturbing features of modern society is the willingness to accept as fact what is read in newspapers, heard on the radio or seen on television. A healthy suspicion of commercially presented information and the habit of substantiating it by reference to alternative sources when important, provides some defence against deception and manipulation while fostering an independence of mind.

Using knowledge

Locating the knowledge required and validating it is only the first step in making use of that information. Information then has to be ordered, analysed and interpreted. At this point the teacher should be looking for a third step – formation of important concepts – as application of knowledge to the solution of problems and the making of decisions takes place.

Not all teachers are as conscious of this third step as perhaps they should be. Children do develop considerable skills at assembling and ordering information but at that point where the information is presented the project or other exercise often comes to an end. To take a simple example: a project on Victorians can finish at the point when – through displays of written work, two- and three-dimensional art, music and craft – the children present their findings about the Victorians. The opportunity to use this knowledge to perhaps make comparisons with various aspects of society today or in the more distant past is often not taken. From these comparisons a variety of concepts such as that of continuity and change, cause and effect, values, power and so on can be developed. Pupils are invited to make judgements and express opinions on education, health care, law and order and other elements of life then and now. Their judgements have to be backed up by the information they have uncovered and analysed.

Thinking critically

By moving into the third level of activity, teachers are helping their children to think critically as a matter of normal practice, to make judgements and to take decisions based on validated facts. It takes little imagination to realise how important this will be when the children grow up and take their places in a society subject to a high degree of persuasion, complex technology, rapid change and an increasingly threatened environment. Making judgements independently based on sound and tested information must surely be a very important skill.

Personal qualities

There is of course another dimension which has to be borne in mind when we are considering skills, knowledge and understandings which will enable an individual to cope with life in the 21st century. The most rational and balanced judgements, based on the best of well-founded information, will be flawed if they do not have at their core a concern for the consequences for other people. History is full of leaders whose judgements were rational and well informed but whose consequent actions ignored the ultimate good of those most affected. Their judgements lacked the elements of compassion and care for others.

It is important – perhaps more important than anything else that children learn in school – that they are taught from the earliest age to place the good of others before that of themselves. It is the hardest of all lessons to learn. It involves the control of selfish instincts and the development of unselfish, caring and considerate behaviour. Schools, with their emphasis on communal life and their opportunities for co-operation and helpfulness, offer a rich setting for developing such qualities. Too often the demand for academic excellence or an over-emphasis on the importance of competition and success at all costs, leaves too little time for the discussion and fostering of the gentler qualities of tenderness, compassion, caring and kindness. A curriculum which does not place priority on the development of such personal qualities has little hope of generating a future society which holds them dear.

Summary

A view of the aims of the primary school curriculum could fall under these five headings:
1 To help the pupil become knowledgeable and skilful in relevant and enriching ways.
2 To give pupils information-gathering skills, including literacy and numeracy, which will enable them to inform themselves as the need arises.
3 To give pupils the skills needed to order, validate, evaluate and interpret information and also to begin to internalise concepts which are vital to good judgement, particularly those which relate to the kind of adult society they are likely to live in.
4 To give pupils opportunities for using information to make rational choices, decisions and judgements. From these activities

to foster the ability to think independently and critically while deepening self-knowledge and understanding of their own emotions and needs.
5 To teach children the importance of encompassing all judgements with consideration for others and to actively promote qualities of tolerance, compassion and kindness.

An opportunity for the small school

If these very general aims are acceptable as one possible outline for a primary curriculum then it becomes interesting to relate them to the nature of the small school. It does appear that such curriculum aims are as obtainable in a small school as in a large one. In some ways the small school may even have an advantage. Secure and long-lasting relationships which at the same time demand co-operation within a wide range of age and ability can encourage responsible attitudes. The teacher's relationship with the child over an extended period offers the chance to foster desirable qualities of tolerance, consideration and kindliness, while the presence of younger children assists in this. The organisation of the mixed age/ability classroom necessitates periods of self-directed activity and this presents an opportunity to encourage the making of independent judgements. Outside the school there is often a rich natural environment where the development of observation and information-gathering skills can go hand in hand with the growth of an understanding of interdependence, stewardship and a wealth of important concepts. It is to this rich educational source we now turn our attention.

Using the environment

'There is too much teaching about the environment and too little teaching from it or for it.' This was the gist of a statement by R. W. Colton, Director of Project Environment 8–18, in the Schools Council Working Paper 55 'The Curriculum in the Middle Years' (Evans/Methuen Educational, 1975). It is a statement with an immediate appeal to those who believe in the importance of the environment not only as a basis for study but also as the crucial factor in the quality of human existence. It is not just an important educational resource but rather the real world in which, when the shelter of home and school are left behind, the individual has to live. Secondary sources have to be relied upon to supply us with some of our information but much is to be learned from the first-hand experience that can only come outside the classroom.

Small schools often seem to 'fit' into their environment in ways which larger institutions do not. In the country the ocean of field and woodland

Curriculum opportunities 63

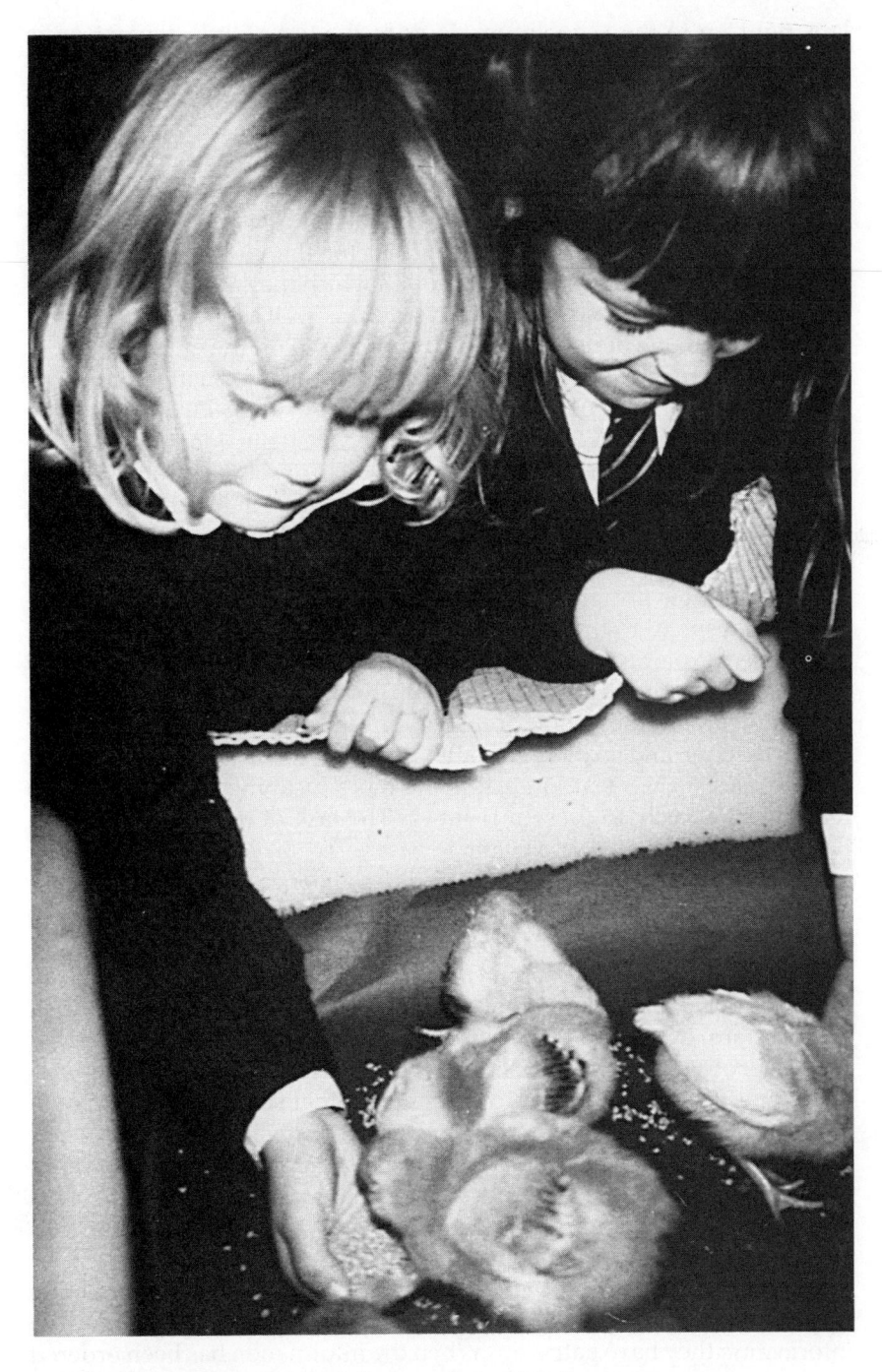

12. The first-hand experience of young, live animals.

laps right up to the schoolroom door; in the town, little separates the small primary school from the street. In both cases, the real world is there just through the window, on the other side of the door, waiting to be explored.

Educating children through the environment responds soundly enough also to the findings of Bruner and Piaget on the way children learn. It pursues a belief that primary school children learn best by active discovery and first-hand experience; that for the most part this is the stage of intellectual development through which they are passing (Figure 12). That it satisfies a need to be physically as well as mentally active at this age is also one of its attractions. Study based on the environment in no way precludes the use of secondary sources of information: indeed it often promotes their use in more meaningful ways. Pictures, books, slides, tapes, radio and television are all used to clarify, identify, evaluate and expand what has been discovered and help in solving problems. The primary and secondary sources of learning go hand in hand in widening perspectives, deepening understanding and enriching experience. Relating environmental learning to the curriculum aims discussed earlier in this chapter, it is not difficult to see how an exploration of the environment can respond to those aims.

Children exploring their immediate environment are encouraged to assimilate knowledge which is relevant to their understanding of that environment. As they come to use their local experience as a base for understanding and explore through secondary sources past times or distant places, their learning can have more meaning for them and be related more easily to present realities. The task of recognising what is pertinent and what is irrelevant is eased. To take but one example, someone who has investigated the interdependence of humans, animals and vegetation in his or her own environment is better placed to understand the global implications of this interdependence.

In the second and third of our curricular aims the value of being able to locate, order, validate and interpret information was stressed. When children are exploring the environment they should be developing powers of observation and skills of recording. There will be opportunities to ask questions. Later the use of books and other sources of information will foster library research and other information-gathering skills. Children can be encouraged to validate their information through reference to other sources and not accept too quickly the first evidence uncovered or presented. A careful interpretation of what the information implies takes the children a step beyond validation.

Too often even the most encouraging, well-planned and stimulating environmental projects fall short of encouraging children to use the information they have gathered. When the information has been ordered and validated it can be used then to make comparisons, form opinions, suggest choices or take decisions. In later sections of this chapter ways are suggested for doing this. From this activity, stemming from first-hand experience of the environment, can be developed a whole range of important concepts, from interdependence and stewardship to the use of power and the understanding of changing values. Qualities of care, tolerance and sensitivity to the needs of others can be fostered.

Simulated classroom models
Warner's Wood

The following brief, simulated exploration of a wood by an imagined two-teacher school serves to illustrate the way in which an environmental study project can pursue the curricular aims already outlined.

Preliminaries

The wood has been visited by the two teachers, its potential noted, plans and sketches made and permission from the owner for a series of school visits obtained.

The teachers have decided to involve all the junior and top infant children in the project. The investigation will be organised around the fostering of five important concepts. The activities involved will encourage the development of information-gathering skills, useful and interesting facts will be encountered and opportunity given for judgements and choices to be made. Aesthetic appreciation and certain personal qualities will be encouraged. A chart showing how the project is expected to develop has been made and is displayed in the classroom.

Organisation

The children have been organised into five groups, each one related to a particular concept. The groups are of mixed age ability. Guide cards suggesting how the children can set about their investigations have been made for each group. There has been a good deal of preliminary discussion with the children about the nature of the project and what it is hoped to achieve.

Concept groups

The five concepts to be considered are:
Interdependence
Stewardship
Power
Alike and different
Quality (i.e. colour, forms, patterns, textures, sounds, shadings)

Interdependence

This group started with an investigation of the food chain and the interdependence of plants, insects and animals. This involved the group in much observation, some collection, library research and the production of flow charts and diagrams with explanatory writing. They made sketches of insects, birds and small animals feeding. A model illustrating the food chain was made for the classroom display.

The group then explored the relationship of man and the woodland. They investigated the present human activity in the wood, which included some thinning for firewood and occasional timber felling for sale; shooting pigeons, pheasant and rabbits; autumn pig feeding and three hives at the wood edge. The children asked questions of the owner, looked for and recorded signs of felling and thinning, sought evidence of hunted animals, sketched the hives, observed the bee flight paths and became interested in the process of pollination. They then looked at the way people had used the wood in the past, at evidence of coppicing, and through secondary material found out the likely use of the woodland in medieval and prehistoric times. They went back to see if there were still edible berries of the type prehistoric men and women may have gathered and discussed whether charcoal burners may have used the wood.

The group then generalised their evidence to look at the importance of the interdependence of humans, animals and vegetation globally.

Stewardship

This group was involved with investigating threats to the wood from people, wild animals and unwanted vegetation. They looked for signs of misuse by people from the leaving of rubbish to the trampling down of plants. The damage caused by rabbits, squirrels and deer was noted and evidence of damage to plants by certain fungi and parasites. This wood was well-managed but there was still evidence of inappropriate planting in the past and harm to the ecological balance. The importance of management to the healthy growth of trees was looked at. The children had briefed themselves to detect some of the more obvious tree diseases and the effects of acid rain. They found none in this case. The children spoke to the owner about the future of the wood, found out what the planning restrictions were and learnt about Tree Preservation Orders.

The children sent for materials from bodies such as the Woodland Trust and other conservation organisations. An investigation back at school made them conscious of the worldwide threat to woodland and forest. A classroom display of drawings, paintings, models, graphs, pictures and writing illustrated these problems locally and globally. The display later went to the village shop when the children decided on a publicity campaign to raise the villagers' awareness of the problem.

Power

The concept of power was a new one to most of this group, or at least they thought so. The power of natural forces was first considered. The children examined evidence in the wood of nature re-establishing itself after damage from animals or humans. They also considered the power of plant life at the base of the food chain and the result of any decline on the animal life of the wood. The way in which the tree cover dictated the type of vegetation beneath, the effect of drought, of too much rain, and many other manifestations of the power of nature, were investigated.

The children also explored the power of animals over one another – especially the hunter over the hunted. Ways in which the hunted defended themselves were examined, which led to an investigation of camouflage, movement and deception. The devices used by the hunters to exercise their power, from spiders' webs to the silent flight of owls, were also carefully considered.

The power of humans over plant and animal life led to an investigation of the human hunter, forester and collector and to parish records to try to discover past ownership of the wood. A visit to a parish council meeting illustrated how local decisions were made and how power was exercised there. The local district councillor was invited to talk to the school about the work of the local authority and the power it exercised. There was further work on decision-making and power within families, schools, communities and nations. The children examined ways in which they exercised power in the family, over pets and so on. A display followed. As well as a collection of items – sketches, pictures and writing – there was a large chart illustrating the structure of decision-making in families, local communities and nations.

Alike and different

This group was looking for contrasts in the wood – for things that were alike in some ways and different in others. The children's investigations first led them into contrasts in the size of plant life, from trees to lichen. Later they did similar work with birds, insects and mammals. This led to an investigation of what were the features that distinguished one form of life from another. The acorn and the oak tree, where difference is obvious and likeness harder to understand, led to an examination of growth and change, where basic likeness is hidden by apparent difference. Nature's purpose in providing differences was looked at in terms of shape, colour, sound and movement. The insect world provided a rich contrast of movement, shape and colour among basically similar creatures. The variation in soil and the vegetation it supported proved interesting, as did the process of ageing in plants. Later, in the classroom, the concept of alike and different was introduced in wider terms to show the basic similarity of needs and hopes among the apparently different peoples of the world. Activities were similar to the other groups, including information-gathering and forms of exposition.

Quality

This group set out to investigate the features that gave the woodland its special quality. The children were looking for and recording by sketch, film and tape recorder the colours, forms, patterns, textures, sounds and shadings that were everywhere within the wood. Colour of flower, pattern of leaf vein, texture of tree bark, sound of bird song were only starting points in an environment bursting with opportunity for this group. The most adventurous expedition with the teacher and three parents was a visit to the wood at 1 a.m. to listen to and record the sounds and sights of the wood at night. Some understanding of the life rhythm of the wood, of the sequence of birth, growth and death which has gone on for so many centuries and which gives the wood its special qualities, began to form for the children. Later, in the classroom they made a collection of musical items, copies of paintings, examples of legends and fairy stories, of tales of Robin Hood and Puck, and other examples of the rich culture associated with woodland life. The collection was displayed with notes, original stories and art in two and three dimensions.

Follow-up

Following the investigations each group of children presented their information to their classmates by display and during a session in which they described their activities and what they had found. The children were given a chance to look at the displays, ask questions, read the notes and stories, listen to recordings and make themselves thoroughly familiar with the work of the other groups. Each of the groups devised a quiz to test informally how much had been learnt. The display was the centrepiece of a parents' evening when group leaders presented their findings to an adult audience.

The teacher extended the project by suggesting that the wood, which was near the village, had been looked at as the site for a new milk products factory. A large national firm had been looking for such a site for some time. The children were asked to present arguments for and against the use of the site in this way. Arguments against destruction of the wood were quickly put forward but children were then asked to consider matters such as employment, a declining school, church and village population, the drift away of young people and how a new factory would help solve these problems. Debates, mock village meetings, publicity material for and against, interviews and the like gave the factory proposal reality. In the end it was supposed that the matter went to a public enquiry. Each child acted as the inspector, weighed the evidence and made a choice. A final vote was taken. (The wood was narrowly saved.)

Summary

Such a project as this involves much that pursues the curricular aims that have been put forward:
1 Children have become more knowledgeable in useful ways.
2 Information-gathering and literacy skills have been used.
3 Information has been ordered, evaluated, validated and used to make judgements and choices.
4 Valuable concepts and aesthetic awareness have been fostered.
5 Sensitivity to the needs of others and other personal and social qualities have been encouraged.

Using the community

It has been suggested that small schools often serve compact and cohesive societies which have a strong sense of community. This is not always so but it is the case often enough for this to present a special curriculum opportunity for many small schools.

The involvement of the community comes perhaps more naturally in the countryside where the school is often sited in the middle of the village. The villagers see the school and hear the children every school day, as they pass it on the way to work or to the village stores. Many will have gone there as children. It is as familiar as the village church or chapel and part of the background of people's lives. If there is a village hall the school may not be the only centre of village life and parish meetings, socials and dances may take place in the hall rather than in the school. Nevertheless the school is part of the consciousness of local people, whether they have children there or not, and even if it is not much used by the community there is normally a great good will towards it.

Many village schools make excellent use of the rich educational resource that a village community represents. There are buildings to explore which can range from an ancient parish church to a tiny cottage. Nearby are farms, and perhaps manor houses, follies and wells, tumuli and ruins. But it is the people and the structure of village life with its annual events and rhythm through the seasons which can be the most rewarding in a social studies project.

The same can be said of some small town schools, especially those which have served a particular part of a town for many years. While not always carrying quite the same loyalties and affection, there can still be strong support for the school and real interest in its activities. On pages 75–80 we look at the remarkable use of a local community to enrich the curriculum made by a small town school. First, though, we look at a social studies project carried through by an imaginary village school which may help point up the opportunities that often exist in villages for this kind of exercise.

Simulated classroom models
Stillwood, a village study

Stillwood is an imaginary village of 1000 inhabitants. It lies six miles from the nearest market town in the centre of farmland mainly devoted to dairy herds and sheep. There is some woodland and a Forestry Commission plantation. Prior to the Industrial Revolution there was a considerable woollen cloth-making industry based in cottages and small water-driven mills. The prosperity of the 16th, 17th and 18th centuries has left its mark in a number of substantial buildings, a fine church and the relics of three small mills. There has been some movement into this pleasant village of professional and business people from the town and many villagers now go daily to the town to work. There is a lively community spirit and the village is supportive of its small four-teacher school to which most of the children go for their primary education.

The school has undertaken a village study as its main project for the term. All the junior children and some older infants have been involved.

Preliminaries

The three teachers involved have spent some time together planning this project and have gathered the source material needed from library, museum and other services. They have also made contact with the local people they wish to involve and have gained all the necessary permissions for visits. The aims and general pattern of the project have been agreed upon jointly but each teacher has taken responsibility for developing certain aspects of it. These relate, where possible, to the special interests, experience and skills of each teacher.

The children have been arranged in mixed age/ability groups. Each group will be involved with one particular aspect of the topic. The teachers each have responsibility for organising the activity of certain groups but are essentially involved in the whole project and available to all the children for advice and guidance. The children have been fully briefed on the nature and purposes of the whole project and are brought together frequently to report on the progress of their groups to the rest of the company.

Aims and purposes

The aims of the project were briefly as follows:
(a) To deepen the children's understanding and appreciation of their own community.
(b) To develop information-gathering skills such as observation, interviewing and library research.
(c) To foster such useful concepts as continuity and change, cause and effect, conflict and consensus.
(d) To give practice in validating information, ordering it and using it to make choices, form opinions and take decisions.
(e) To encourage personal qualities such as an independence of mind, objectivity, openness to new ideas, respect for the opinions of others, empathy, a respect for evidence.

Grouping

The titles of the six groups into which the children were organised were:
People
Homes
Public places
Past and present
Village life
Leisure

Group One: People

The children in this group looked at the lives of people who played a significant part in the day-to-day life of the village. Pupils interviewed the vicar and the Methodist minister, the headteacher, the sub-postmistress and postman, the shopkeeper, the garage-owner who was also the bus proprietor, a housewife, a forester, a farmer whose farm was on the edge of the village, a district councillor, the chairman of the parish council and a businessman who was also a Justice of the Peace. Apart from interviewing these people the children were allowed to spend a day with some of them – with the shopkeeper, the postman, the forester, the vicar and minister and the sub-postmistress. They returned with notes, pictures, sketches, tape recordings, pamphlets and articles of various sorts. From this they built up a good display to show the activities of all these people. Later a number of these folk were invited to the school to see the exhibition and to talk to the rest of the children about their activities. The children then began to investigate the roles similar people would have played in the village in the past: in what ways these roles had changed or remained the same. They looked also for people who would have been important to the village in the past but had now disappeared.

At this point they began to work closely with the 'Past and present' group.

Later, based on the evidence they had collected, they were asked to compare the work of these different people, to decide whose work they thought most important or interesting and to say why they thought this.

Group Two: Homes

This was a more familiar assignment title. However, it involved the children in trying to group the village houses first by the materials used in building, then by style of construction and then by date. They soon became familiar with the building materials and learnt to distinguish between older traditional materials and modern substitutes. It took longer to recognise the basic characteristics of traditional building styles and put rough dates to the houses. They were able to make their dating more precise in some cases where co-operative house owners had access to deeds.

Having thoroughly investigated the homes in their own village, the children began comparisons with village homes of other areas. By using travel magazines, reference books and holiday brochures they were able to identify different building styles in different parts of the country. The dependence of these styles in past times on the materials available in those places were looked at in terms of cause and effect. The similarity caused by ubiquitous modern materials for building was noted. The children then began to identify the amenities of a modern home, home life in their grandparents' time and then, in a series of steps, what home life may have been like at various times in the past. They sought evidence to verify what they learnt and were asked to identify aspects of continuity and change. Later they were asked to balance the advantages and disadvantages that homes in the village had possessed in the past and have now. Each child was asked to choose a time in the past which they felt would have been interesting to live in and say why they thought this. The group's display included reports, descriptions, drawings, plans, photographs, a photocopy of the deeds of a house, examples of building materials and models of houses.

Group Three: Public places

This group investigated the past and present use of public buildings, and for the sake of this exercise this included the Elizabethan manor house which belongs now to the National Trust and is open to the public. The church offered an excellent starting place and there was much to discover from its building, its furnishings, its monuments and records. The clues to its changing ritual and denominational emphasis were there to discover, as were the indications of the underlying continuity of

Christian worship. The skill of craftsmen and the love and support of parishioners were evidenced everywhere.

From the parish church the children went on to investigate the Methodist chapel, the manor house, the Jubilee Hall, the school, the ruins of the old mills, the Green Dragon Inn and the history of open public spaces such as the village playing field and the 'Commons'. The people involved in the management and life of these places were informative and helpful and the group's displays reflected this. The group also brought their information together in a small booklet called 'The Public Places of Stillwood' which, with some editing and additional material, was accepted by the parish council as the basis for a new village pamphlet using the same title.

Group Four: Past and present

This group were to concentrate on the history of the village and to make some comparisons with present life there. Their research led them to local historians, the county archivist and to many interviews with older villagers. They used reference materials to get an impression of the nature of villages such as theirs through different periods in history and then searched their own village for confirmation of that impression. Early and recent Ordnance Survey maps illustrated the growth of the village over the last century, while reference to the county archives through the museum service produced one or two older maps of the area. Records held by the parish clerk and the vicar proved informative about occupations, standards of living, poverty and wealth. The churchyard gave some indication of family size, life expectation and attitudes.

When the children had gathered as much information as they reasonably could from these and other sources, they were asked to arrange displays which would indicate what they thought the village may have been like at four particular points in history.

The displays included descriptions, stories, models, paintings, taped music indicative of the period and a collection of items loaned by local people or the museum service. There was some emphasis on copies of actual documents and records. The children also made a collection of suitable fiction which related to these various periods and read two of these books aloud as a group. They compared the English language as it was written in the 12th, 14th and 16th centuries. They found out about mummers' plays and put on a very simple version of their own as a conclusion to their part of the project.

Group Five: Village life

This group set out to look at contemporary village life. They were interested in its institutional life rather than that of individuals whose activities had been studied by Group One. They found out how the village was governed, who made decisions, how health care and education were provided, who cared for the old, how influential the religious life of the village was and how all kinds of social and communication services were provided. When statutory bodies had been examined then the children turned to the work of local voluntary bodies and their part in securing and enriching the life of the community. Conservation organisations and those concerned with planning were among these. Both statutory and voluntary bodies welcomed the interest of these future citizens and went to great trouble to provide them with information and first-hand experience of how their organisations operated.

Some of the children were allowed to attend a meeting of the Parish Council and the Parochial Church Council. The teacher then took a group of four older children to sit in on a meeting of the District Council in the town. The children found out a good deal about the way in which a number of voluntary organisations helped to care for the village community, particularly the old, the very young, the sick and the troubled.

The group's display was called 'Who Cares for Our Village?' and it included descriptions, charts, pictures, pamphlets and much else which illustrated the communal life of the village and the work of the statutory and voluntary bodies which sustained it.

The children were finally challenged to detail ways in which they could enhance the quality of life in the village. They soon found a whole range of useful activities that the school could participate in from a litter-scavenge on the playing field to shopping for the housebound.

Group Six: Leisure

This group found much more to explore and investigate than they at first supposed. The obvious starting places were the village football and cricket teams. There was much to record there and a host of statistics and photographs to examine. They found that there were several more teams in the village – a bowls side, a skittles team and a darts team. When they questioned individuals they found that some young men played rugby for the town side, and many people played tennis or went swimming at the town pool. Some fished and a number of farmers rode to hounds.

The children then turned away from sport and looked at the many fellowships and organisations that the village supported. There was the WI, the Mothers Union, Scouts, Cubs and Guides, the Church Youth Club, a Ramblers' Club, a branch of the British Legion and a number of other societies and clubs linked to special interests and hobbies.

The group then turned its attention to the pattern of people's holidays and found out where people went and why. Lastly they concerned themselves with the traditional events of the village: the annual Sports

Day, the fete and the Christmas concert. Stretching back over many more years were the festivals connected to the church: Christmas, Harvest and Easter. This led to an examination of how people spent their leisure in times past. Interviews with older villagers turned up some fascinating information on leisure pursuits and past customs. One of these, the maypole dance, the school decided to revive.

The children used their information to draw contrasts with the past and with leisure pursuits in a town, to examine the effect of developments like television or the coming of the travelling library on village social life. The children made some attempt to predict how people may spend their spare time in the future and what the advances of technology might produce. All their findings were communicated in a display called 'Leisure Time in Stillwood'. It proved one of the most popular displays.

Conclusions

During the unfolding of the project and the building-up of the displays, the groups regularly reported their progress back to the other children. When they had finally completed their work, each group made a full presentation to the class and arranged an 'Any Questions' session, with themselves as the experts. An 'Open Evening' was arranged and many villagers came to see the displays and hear the children talk about their investigations.

The teachers felt that the project had achieved many of its purposes and identified the following areas as being particularly successful:

1 The children had learnt a great deal more about their village, its people and its past.
2 They had used a wide range of information-gathering skills and had done much purposeful reading and writing.
3 They had encountered such concepts as power, continuity and change, cause and effect, and deepened other understandings.
4 They had been challenged with making choices, stating opinions and taking decisions (all based on the information they had collected, ordered and validated) and communicating them.
5 They had experienced a little of the vigorous activity and rich heritage which waits to be enjoyed in many communities by those who participate fully in their society.
6 They had co-operated with and supported each other, listened to each other's opinions and learnt to respect them.

★

'Neighbours', an inner-city study

Hornersvale is a district in the inner area of a large city. A once flourishing community linked to local factories, its prosperity has declined as the traditional manufacturing base has withered. Two small factories still prosper and parts of the district reflect this but there is a good deal of unemployment, some shops are boarded up, there are poorly cleared factory sites lying derelict and the area suffers more than its share of vandalism and petty crime. However, there is much bustling and colourful life which reflects the varied ethnic roots of the population. There are large differences in the cultural, religious and language backgrounds of the 90 children who attend the local school. It is one of the few small inner city schools in the authority and once catered for a much larger school population. However, transport to the next school is considered long and hazardous across a number of the city's most congested streets and this has saved the school from closure.

The headteacher is a well-known and popular figure locally and draws her school into community activity and the community into the school when she sees this to be of benefit. Although housed in an old building the school is bright, warm and welcoming. There has long been a policy of openness and there is ready access for those who want to offer help in the school, or who want to use it for community activities. For many years the building itself has been the only meeting place for people, other than the church hall, and its importance in this respect has increased as the variety of religious backgrounds locally has grown.

The school decided to undertake a neighbourhood study and chose to call it 'Neighbours'. The project involved the two junior classes and the older infants.

Preliminaries

The teachers involved did a considerable amount of preliminary work not only in assembling materials and information but in visits to people, groups and establishments likely to be involved in the study. They were generally successful in gaining permission for the children to make visits, undertake interviews, ask questions and collect the information and materials they needed.

The teachers jointly produced a project plan and each had an area of special responsibility as well as a general commitment. A large wall chart showing how the project was expected to develop was made and used as a centrepiece in explaining to the children what the study was about. The local secondary school made a short video of the district showing some unexpected views of the neighbourhood which did much to whet the children's curiosity.

Aims

(a) To increase the children's knowledge of their neighbourhood and to develop positive, caring and socially helpful attitudes to the diver-

sity of cultural, religious and ethnic backgrounds among the local population.
(b) To foster an awareness, sensitivity and appreciation of the variety of visual art, music and language that exist in the neighbourhood.
(c) To encourage the understanding of concepts such as interdependence, alike and different, stewardship, power and responsibility and how they relate to the quality of life in the neighbourhood.
(d) To develop literacy and information-gathering skills, interpretative, ordering and validation skills.
(e) To present opportunities for the children to make some choices and decisions based on information they have ordered and validated.
(f) To involve parents and local people in the project as much as possible; provide an opportunity for greater understanding among diversity; foster the growth of a stronger sense of community; and encourage an awareness of interdependence and the need for mutual support.

Groupings

The children were arranged in six mixed age/ability groups. The teachers allowed the children a limited amount of choice as to the group they joined but tried to ensure that each group had children from various ethnic groups within it. There were about 12 children in each group. Each teacher had a responsibility for two groups and an aspect of the project which was his/her special province.

The titles of the groups into which the children were organised are as follows:
Many neighbours
Neighbours at home
Neighbours at work
Good neighbours
Neighbours at ease
Unexpected neighbours

Group A: Many neighbours

The children in this group were involved in exploring the origins of the different ethnic groups which were to be found in the neighbourhood. This entailed a number of interviews with older and younger people. Among the older members were many who had lived originally in another country and who were able to tell the children a great deal about life there. This enriched and motivated studies of these other countries by the children. A large map showing how people had come to this country and where they had come from was produced; pictures and many objects from these other lands were loaned. The emphasis was on social and cultural rather than industrial or commercial life.

The children then looked at the movement into this country of groups of people from the earliest times, where they had come from and probable reasons for their coming. The similarities and differences in reasons for migrating and the problems of settlement faced by earlier and later groups of immigrants were seen in the context of the common origin of everyone in this country as a descendant of an immigrant group.

A display was built up of charts, maps, pictures, illustrations, written and taped interviews, written articles, books, clothes and objects, all related to the various countries and groups studied.

Group B: Neighbours at home

This group were concerned with the homes of the local people and the family life within them. Among the topics pursued was a study of the sorts of houses in the area, the dates when they were built, who built them and why, the materials used, the changing style of building and its relation to changing needs and expectations. The children found differences in the way people furnished their houses, the types of food they prepared and ate, the importance given to mealtimes and in the daily routine of the home. The varying demands made upon the children of the family in helping around the home and the way family decisions were made gave the children a deeper insight into varying concepts of responsibility, duty and the exercise of authority.

The willingness of families to allow the pupils into the privacy of their homes varied but teachers were careful to ensure that nothing that was written or said could be hurtful. The group's display included reports, descriptions, taped conversations, photographs, recipes, food and objects from the homes.

Group C: Neighbours at work

This group looked at the various jobs that people in the neighbourhood did. The group undertook surveys, made charts, visited shops, factories and offices, interviewed a variety of people, and made a tape called 'Working City' which recorded the sounds of the city at work. A variety of people were invited to the school to talk about their jobs, a few of whom gave some preliminary instruction to the children. Photographs were taken, sketches and paintings were made and tools and instruments that are used in the various occupations were loaned. The children completed their part of the project by looking back at the main occupations of the district in past centuries, at change and continuity. Their efforts built into an interesting and colourful display.

Group D: Good neighbours

This group examined the activities of services, voluntary and statutory, which support the community in various ways. Some of the children listed and found out about the uniformed services – the fire, police, ambulance, nursing and traffic warden services. They paid visits, wrote reports, interviewed officers and invited them to the school. Photographs were taken and some interesting tape recordings were made. The services were willing to loan objects and items of uniform for display with posters and literature. One fire officer agreed to act as a model in his full fire-fighting uniform for some life drawing and painting – the first time the children had tried this type of art. Two of the group attempted a three-dimensional representation in clay. The community policeman, already a regular visitor to the school, brought the police dog and handler for a demonstration.

The remainder of the children looked for the help given by non-uniformed services, many of them voluntary. The list was long and the children found out a little about the work of such diverse bodies as the Samaritans and the Water Board. They also found out about the voluntary help given to the very old or infirm, to the housebound or handicapped, to youth clubs and playgroups. Again there were visits to be made, interviews to conduct, questions to ask, reports to write, sketches and paintings to make. The whole grew into an attractive display.

Group E: Neighbours at ease

The children sought out the ways in which people of the area entertained themselves and their involvement in community activity. They found out about local sports teams, hobbies and the societies and clubs which were popular. Their look at fellowships led them to the church, mosque, temple and synagogue. Some of the basic differences in religious practice were touched upon but generally these were felt to be deserving of a fuller study in depth at a later date. The furnishings of these religious buildings and their decoration led to a search for contrasts in style, colour and pattern. There followed then a look at the various traditions in art, music, dance and literature flowing from the different ethnic backgrounds. Copies, rubbings and tape recordings were made. Models and plans were made of the various religious buildings. The children attempted decoration and patterns in the styles of the various traditions and listened to and tried the various instruments.

Group F: Unexpected neighbours

Wild life is unexpected in the inner city but in fact often abounds in parks or any overgrown open space. With the help of a local naturalist the children explored the mini-beast world of overgrown factory sites. An abundance of insects, spiders, butterflies and moths was found while the bird life proved surprisingly plentiful and varied. The children bred frog-spawn and released the young frogs into damp areas beside a stream; they recorded for the park keeper the numbers and types of ducks on the park ponds; they made and put up nesting-boxes in the school grounds in places well hidden from vandals. They looked for and found signs of urban foxes, hedgehogs, mice and voles. The variety of wild flowers and plants growing on the derelict sites surprised even the teachers. Recordings, sketches, reports, track casts, collections and pictures all added to the final display.

Conclusions

The children had been kept in touch with what other groups had undertaken throughout the project by presentations, displays and 'Any Questions' sessions. Their group work often concluded with challenges to suggest how improvements could be made and problems overcome, and this involved both choice- and decision-making.

The children ended their project with a 'Neighbourhood Evening' at the school. Blessed with a little extra space, the displays were set out attractively. Parents and friends were invited to see the displays, listen to music and watch dances which reflected the district's rich cultural diversity. Parents who had helped with the project and others were invited to wear traditional dress and to bring along traditional food. Some adults also contributed to the music-making and dance. The project was considered to have been generally successful as a sampling of the district's educational potential and revealed a number of areas for more detailed study.

The children certainly knew a little more about their local community and environment; they had extended their general knowledge, had practised a wide range of learning skills, had been encouraged to interpret and use the information gathered to make choices and been given opportunity for both creative and aesthetic experience. The group work had demanded co-operation, leadership and consensus. Many adults in the district had been brought together with an opportunity to learn a little more about their neighbours' traditions and to enjoy a communal activity together.

The three simulated projects 'Warner's Wood', 'Stillwood – a village study' and '"Neighbours" – an inner city study' are outlined not only to suggest a possible approach to the use of the environment and the local community for educational purposes but also to illustrate the opportunities which lie open to both urban and rural small schools when eyes are lifted above the school gates. Often, though not always, the small size of the school gives it a special and intimate association with the small population it serves. That relationship can be used to great benefit by the school, and where the school throws itself wholeheartedly into the life of the community it can enrich communal life also. An actual example of this involvement of a small school in the community is described in chapter 6.

Project approach

In the examples above the study of the social and natural environments has been developed through what is generally known as the 'project' method. In primary schools it is generally accepted that 'doing a project' means selecting a particular topic, theme or centre of interest and through a variety of activities – and often across subject boundaries – pursuing certain aims and objectives similar to those already outlined. It may be helpful to review at this point some of the preliminary actions and organisational tasks which can help to make a project more successful. They are not exhaustive and some projects are far less satisfactory than others. What is important is to analyse at the end of every project what went well and what did not, put aside discouragement and believe experience improves the prospects of success.

Preparation

1 Leave enough time. Hurried planning is rarely good planning. Know what next term's themes will be *this* term.
2 Order books and resources in good time. Delivery is often slow and projects are unlikely to succeed without appropriate resources. Seek out the catalogues of the schools museum service, the schools library service, the county film library and any other resource bank that the authority maintains.
3 Check that materials and tools are ready before each lesson. Train the children to collect and return materials without reference to you. Trust them. Too much teacher time is lost by teachers delving and delivering themselves.

Organisation

1 Group the children. In small schools this will normally be in groups of mixed ability and age.
2 Prepare a number of guide cards for each group, indicating the areas of investigation they are to follow and the procedure for

doing it. The guide cards should allow for the variation of age and ability by providing a wide range of challenge and allowing for varied levels of response. The guide cards should be open-ended and not confining – launching pads not ladders.

3 Provide each group with a large folder for all its work. Desks and trays are not the best place to keep paintings and charts. Have a central storage point for the folders.

4 Rooms should be arranged as workshops, not as lecture theatres. The layouts suggested in chapter 1 lend themselves to project work. There should ideally be positions for quiet work such as reading and writing, libraries for book research, a variety of practical bays – including those for science and maths experiment – and a small group-teaching area.

The project plan

Having made sure that the topic fits into the overall programme of the school, a written plan should be made. The plan could include the following sections.

1 *The aims* of the project, perhaps under these sub-headings:
   (a) Central purpose of the project.
   (b) An indication of the main body of knowledge to be learnt.
   (c) An indication of the learning skills to be developed.
   (d) What major concepts it is hoped to illuminate.
   (e) The social and personal qualities to be fostered.
   (f) The aesthetic experiences to be provided.

2 *The structure* of the project, which will show the following:
   (a) The areas of study that are to be covered and how the theme will be developed. This is most simply done in the form of a flow chart or diagrammatic net.
   (b) The chart can also indicate the concept areas to be encountered.
   (c) The chart can be displayed on the classroom wall to allow the children to follow the project's progress.
   (d) There will be spaces on the chart to allow for new areas to be added.
   (e) The chart can be designed so that it is a pictorial illustration of the project theme.
   (f) It is useful to use different-coloured card for the charts each year; this makes filing and retrieval simpler.
   (g) Details of the project's aims and intended development can be written on the back of the chart.
   (h) Finally, when the project is finished, a short evaluation of its

strengths and weaknesses can be added on the back of the chart, which is then filed for possible further use.

Session pattern

The pattern of the lessons when the project is being undertaken may vary but it can be productive if the groups are organised as follows:
1. The children are brought together at the start of each session. A little is said about the project's progress so far, and what is going to happen that day is discussed. From time to time some new item – a picture, slides or an artefact perhaps – is introduced to stimulate interest in the project and arouse enthusiasm before the children set out on their own investigations that day.
2. The children are encouraged to hold their own planning sessions within their groups to make sure that everyone is being properly supported and knows what he/she is doing.
3. The groups report back at regular intervals to the whole class on their progress.
4. When the project is completed, each group makes a major presentation about its part of the project. Group members use their display, arrange a quiz, act as an 'Any Questions' panel of experts, devise competitions and generally make sure that everyone in the class knows what they have done.

The display

This is a very important part of most projects and it is well worth taking trouble over. The following suggestions may be helpful:
   (a) Let the display grow as the project develops.
   (b) Ensure quality. Display paintings, models and three-dimensional art on good backgrounds; use draped material as a backing and to link wall and shelf displays.
   (c) Let the children make booklets suitable for display and allow them to work to their own format rather than use exercise books.
   (d) Keep unfinished models away from the display.
   (e) Keep the display together, not scattered around the room.
   (f) Have clear captions.
   (g) Involve the children in mounting the display. When, and if, they become skilled enough, allow them to plan it and mount it alone.
   (h) Keep a proper balance between material made by the children

and published or teacher-made information sheets and pictures. Both are needed.
(i) Use the display as a teaching aid – refer to it often. Have written questions or comments as captions on the display to stimulate interest and discussion.

Content

Projects will offer opportunities to learn facts, develop many kinds of skills, foster valuable personal qualities and encourage worthwhile attitudes.

Factual content

It can be argued that there will be a body of factual knowledge that it will be desirable for a child leaving the primary school to have; that without those facts the child may be disadvantaged in later stages of education. Deciding what that body of facts should be is extremely difficult and inevitably involves some value judgements by the teachers who draw up the curriculum. Even a centrally decided curriculum is more likely to be concerned with concepts and skills than with facts. With so much to choose from and with knowledge being added to and becoming outdated so rapidly it is only possible here to make the following suggestions:

(a) Ensure that the facts to be learnt are selective and absorbable. Often too many facts are presented.
(b) See that the information is relevant and interesting.
(c) Make sure that it supports the concepts being fostered and is an appropriate vehicle for the skills being learnt.
(d) Ensure that the inclusion of particular facts can be justified in clear terms.

Language content

Thematic work offers great opportunity for the use of relevant, well-motivated oral and written language work for a wide range of purposes. There are many situations which can lead the children into using language, for example for recording, reporting, generalising, explaining, expressing opinions, regulating, justifying, presenting arguments, persuading, speculating, projecting, reflecting, expressing feelings, story telling, writing poetry.

It does not take too much imagination to see how a project such as 'Warner's Wood' could lend itself to using language for some of these purposes.

Skill content: information-gathering skills

Apart from the practice of the basic literacy skills of reading and writing, projects offer great opportunities for developing skill in information-gathering. Information can be gathered from primary or secondary sources and it is convenient to look at them under these headings.

Using primary sources

Careful observation.
Learning to look for clues (in a village study, for example, noting alterations to the cottages, the war memorial as an indication of population, street signs, etc.).
Techniques for note-taking during field work and collecting.
Techniques for interviewing people (the preliminary letter, the preparation of questions, the introductory chat).
If tape recording, the importance of eye-contact, microphone position, etc.

Using secondary sources

Library skills.
Using the catalogue, filing system, Dewey classification.
Using books – previewing, the contents list, skimming, scanning, using opening sentences of paragraphs, using the appendix, glossary, bibliography, etc.
Using an atlas (underestimated as an information source), use of gazetteer.
Reading flow charts, histograms, graphs, bar graphs, pie charts, clock graphs, distance charts.
Using the microcomputer (increasingly important as an information source).
Other secondary sources such as slides, radio or video tapes, TV.
Gaining and clarifying information through experimentation, dramatisation and simulation.

It is of course important to give some preliminary training and explanation before these skills are used by the children in their projects.

Skill content: interpretative skills

Gathering information is one thing; interpreting it so that it can be used is quite another. We all know knowledgeable people who are not wise, and clever folk who act foolishly. Too often schools fail to grasp the opportunity to let pupils use the information they have gathered. There is another set of skills to be learnt. Among these are the following:

(a) Ordering and classifying information.
(b) Validating information. It is important that children test information and authenticate sources where possible.
(c) Evaluating and interpreting information. Seeking patterns and clues to less obvious implications.
(d) Hypothesising and generalising from the information gathered.
(e) Using verified information to express opinions and make choices, decisions and informed judgements.

From the practice of these skills it would be hoped that children could develop the habit of independent, critical thought. Mass communication and techniques of manipulation put enormous power into the hands of those who control or have access to the media. It will be very important for these children, when they become adults, to be able to sift, test and evaluate information in order to make sound, objective judgements, to think critically about what is presented to them and communicate their opinions.

Concept content

Project work offers the chance to foster a whole range of important concepts. The Schools Council publication, *Time, Space and Society* (Collins), suggests the following as being important: cause and effect; similarity and difference; continuity and change; power; values; conflict and consensus. To these may be added stewardship and interdependence. Teachers will have others to add to this short list.

Social and personal development

Project work encourages the use of group activity which can be helpful in the fostering of social and personal development. Socially the activities can be structured to encourage co-operation, leadership, an understanding of consensus, respect for the opinions of others, openness to new ideas, tolerance, empathy – and a sensitivity to the needs of others which may one day become true compassion. If the content of the projects encourages such concepts as interdependence, this too will play a part in social development.

As the children take increasing responsibility for their activities – and small schools are well placed to encourage this – they can become more self-aware and understanding of their own worth, conscious of their own strengths and able to cope with their own frailties.

Aesthetic development

There will be many chances within most projects to explore aesthetic experience. The music, art, dance, drama and literature of other places and other times as well as our own contemporary culture are all there to explore in appropriate ways. Too often a project investigating a distant country or a distant time will dwell upon physical geography, industry, wars and political figures while neglecting the cultural or spiritual aspects of that time or place.

In creative terms, opportunity for work in two- and three-dimensional art, music-making, drama and dance will usually abound, but teachers need to be alert to their value and seek them out. The temptation to allow excessive copying of pictures from textbooks should give way to drawing from direct observation with crayons and pencils (hard and soft) which allow for shading, and balance the use of felt pens.

Co-operation

Co-operating on a thematic project with colleagues can help teachers to bring more resources, expertise and flexibility to bear. Planning together can bring new ideas while widening horizons and perceptions. Many teachers in small schools are involved in this type of co-operation both within their own schools and with teachers from other schools. It will repay investigation by those not yet involved.

Examples of current practice

A primary school

This small two-teacher school provides an example of an imaginative use of the environment not only to enrich the curriculum but also to overcome the isolation of its children and to benefit other schools.

The school is situated in the countryside about 10 miles from a market town and a little nearer the coast. Within easy walking distance is a variety of farms, hedgebanks, ancient woodlands, plantations, ponds, streams, a rural market, a country church and a manor house belonging to the National Trust.

The school was built between the wars to a standard design which produced rather small classrooms and large cloakrooms. Part of that cloakroom space has been made into additional teaching accommodation. In the early 1980s the number on roll dropped, in common with many primary schools. Pupil numbers began to reach a point where closure or amalgamation could not be entirely discounted. However, it was the matter of very small peer groups, isolation, underuse of facilities and the other associated problems of very small numbers that concerned staff and advisers. The school had good accommodation, spacious school grounds and above all was situated in this varied and rich natural environment.

The potential of the school as a possible base for environmental studies was considered by the head and advisers. The school had established good contacts with local farmers and landowners which could form the basis for development. After some discussion and planning it was decided to set the school up as a base from which urban schools could explore the countryside and other features of the area. There were a number of town schools not too far away for which the organisation of a day in the country would be greatly simplified if they had a base from which to work, some prepared materials made available and access to places of interest prearranged.

Development

The main responsibility for developing the project fell upon the school staff, particularly the head, but encouragement and help was also received from the LEA. Suitable nature trails were outlined and access to woodlands, streams, ponds and hedgerows approved. Local farmers and landowners proved co-operative and arrangements were made to include a variety of farms in the visits.

The preparation of booklets which would indicate the location and nature of the places to be explored went ahead. A collection of suitable reference material was started which eventually included slides and film as well as printed material. Equipment which could be used by visiting schools during their stay was also purchased.

The project has continued to develop. The school is now recognised as an Environmental Studies Centre and is of considerable importance to the area. Schools are now encouraged to camp in the school grounds and use its facilities for short residential visits. The following brief description of the resources held and the activities which can be followed give some idea of how successful the enterprise has been.

Resources

– A parabolic reflector for recording bird song, along with good-quality tape recorders.
– An ultra-violet moth trap and small mammal traps.
– Track- and bark-casting materials. Sweep nets and pond-dipping equipment.
– Tree study equipment: clinometers, callipers, etc.
– Ten pairs of binoculars.
– Compasses and local maps.

- Specimen tubes and minispectors.
- A variety of worksheets and information packs.
- Waterproof capes.

Few individual schools would hold such a variety of environmental studies equipment and these resources are well used.

Topics

The following are suggested in the Centre's pamphlet:
(a) *Trees and woodlands* The school grounds contain both broadleafed and conifer trees while nearby are substantial natural woodlands and plantations. Within the grounds of the nearby National Trust house are more exotic specimens. The school has a nursery for seedling trees.
(b) *Birds* The area is rich in bird life. Bird tables and nesting boxes have been sited in suitable locations in the school grounds. The reflector can be used to record bird song. Some of the farms keep ornamental fowl, while the lake of the manor house has a permanent hide to observe a heronry and water fowl.
(c) *Mammals* Badgers, hares, foxes and red deer live in the nearby woods.
(d) *Farms* Visits to farms can include a demonstration of spinning and natural dyeing. A rural auction market takes place weekly.
(e) *Water* There is a pond in the school grounds and a wide variety of ponds and streams in the district to afford water habitats for study.
(f) *Wild flowers, butterflies and moths* The school has planted a number of bushes which attract moths and butterflies and the ultra-violet moth trap is used at night. The great hedgebanks of north Devon and the woodlands and meadows afford a great variety of flowers.
(g) *Archaeology* There are tumuli and a regular activity is a flint hunt on a nearby farm where flint tools and arrowheads can be found.
(h) *Historic buildings* Nearby there are country churches and churchyards, the local National Trust manor house and local buildings and building materials.

The school grounds and a nearby field have also been set out as an orienteering course. It provides exercises at two levels of difficulty and 20 different permutations of the course which can be followed at the same time.

Comment

It was felt worth while to describe the development of this school environmental study centre in some detail. The school has benefited greatly from the resources and improved access to the environment. The children meet a variety of visiting children and play some part in hosting them. The isolation of staff is also eased. Other schools have gained a valuable new facility.

A final comment

In chapter 6 we see how one school makes full use of community links to enrich the curriculum. In the last few pages we have seen how schools can make use of the real world as well as the one brought to us through books and other sources of information. I have spent some time on this because it does seem to me that there are too many teachers afraid to venture outside the school walls. Indeed there are some so confined by bricks and mortar and a rigid timetable that the descent of a spaceship into the school field would only result in a demand that the children pay attention to their books rather than the little green men walking across the playground.

Small schools, because they are easier to gather together, can venture outside as a complete unit so much more freely. I could gather together my 40 children at North Lew and by calling up the village bus company and two or three parents, take off for Runnymede and Windsor. At Bluecoat it was a major logistical exercise to get the 400 plus juniors across the town to church. Even if small schools can't muster much of a school orchestra (although at least everyone is in it), or put on a sophisticated musical, they can all go to the theatre together. Some small schools now have the best of both worlds: they can take part in the large orchestras, sports teams and concerts which are the results of the co-operative activity of a group of schools, and yet still maintain their independence to initiate visits or other activities themselves.

The ability to react to one-off events was illustrated to me by the numerous centenaries that flourished in the 1970s reflecting the Act providing for popular education. The village schools transformed themselves, it seemed by the dozen, into Victorian classrooms with Sir or Miss becoming almost unrecognisable in period costume. But it doesn't need a centenary to turn a small school into a galleon or a jungle, as has already been said. I'm told of the children of one school who turned themselves into characters from fiction to support a Book Day which drew in the library service. Perhaps most memorable of all was a small school in Devon where the children ran the school for a day. They prepared lessons and taught them, cooked the lunch, cleaned the school and manned the office. The written and illustrative material that came from the preparation for the day and from reflection by the children later on of their experiences, was quite remarkable and of the highest quality – and what fun they had.

It would be foolish to claim that such experiences are exclusive to small schools but it can be claimed that they lend themselves with greater ease to such activities involving the whole school. It is really a matter of taking advantage of the small number of pupils involved and the small number of teachers who have to agree on what is to be done. It is salutary to remember, however, that if one teacher in a very small school isn't willing to go along with the idea, then that can mean 50% of the staff isn't willing and there is no other teacher to turn to – but life is rarely perfect even in small schools.

4 The headteacher's role

The first letter that drops through the box addressed to a new headteacher brings with it a special kind of excitement but the waiting silence of the first assembly or the challenge of the first crisis brings quite a different sort of flutter to the heart. The structure of the British school gives the headteacher a considerable power and status, both legal and perceived; that same structure also creates an isolation and responsibility which all heads have to accept and cope with.

The fact that headteachers in Britain have a legal responsibility for much of what happens in their schools is only partly responsible for this. One of the other reasons is the extensive hierarchy of promotion that now exists in our schools, which has largely grown up since the end of the Second World War. The head now sits on a pyramid of promotion that goes through five scales of teacher plus deputy headteacher. In large schools in particular it is not easy to see the head as a leader among professional equals. The differentials of salary, as well as the intervening promoted posts, create gulfs which heads have to work hard to overcome. In other European countries where the level of all teachers' salaries is more akin to other professions and where there are fewer intermediate promoted posts the isolation of the head seems less marked. A purely subjective view may hold that the round tables found in the conference rooms of some German schools is a symptom of this greater acceptance of a collegiate responsibility: King Arthur sits no higher than the rest of the knights.

Whatever the rights or wrongs of the British system it is the one that exists and has to be lived with. Although the hierarchy in a small school is obviously less elaborate, responsibility for all that happens in the school will still focus on the head. Indeed, when he or she is less protected by senior and administrative staff, that responsibility can be more directly and immediately felt. It is not inconsiderable, even in very small schools. There may be responsibility for the education and welfare of 40 children, the activities of full-time and part-time professional colleagues, half a dozen cleaning, mealtime and kitchen staff, responding to the expectations of up to 80 parents and a board of school governors. Curriculum, buildings, supplies, resources all have to be catered for with perhaps a half-day a week free of a full-time teaching commitment. It is not a quiet life and all who have experienced headship in both large and small schools will know that both are equally demanding in their own particular ways.

It is perhaps convenient to comment on the role of a headteacher in a small school under the following headings:

The head as leader
The head as administrator
The head and curriculum policy
The head and staff
The head as evaluator
The head and other schools
The head and the community.

These roles are overlapping and interact with each other but they do indicate zones of operation even if these are not exclusive.

The head as leader

The head is fulfilling a different role when he or she is acting as leader rather than as chief administrator. Consider this statement in 1964 by Lipham:

'We may define leadership as the initiation of a new structure or procedure for accomplishing an organization's goals and objectives or for changing an organization's goals or objectives. Note that the emphasis here is on initiating change ... The administrator on the other hand, may be identified as the individual who utilizes existing structures or procedures to achieve an organizational goal or objective.'

The leader may be said to be disruptive to the existing state of affairs while the administrator may be seen as a stabilising force. All heads fill both these roles at different times but there is a distinction which it is as well to be aware of.

When as leader the head is initiating change, two routes lie open. One is to use authority as legal head of the institution to insist on certain action being taken and changes made. At times this may be the only way to get the development desired but many headteachers hesitate to use this authority too overtly even when major changes to the school organisation are needed, when new teaching styles are called for or if an important remodelling of the curriculum is necessary. Experience proves to most headteachers that their staff possess a good deal of autonomy within their own classrooms and that insistence on change is a deal away from the successful achievement of that change unless teachers themselves are convinced of its value.

A far more common and successful route to innovation will lie in the exertion of influence and persuasion, of demonstration and through respect for the head's own prestige and achievements. This respect results partly from the built-in authority of the post but more fundamentally it has to be earned.

In a small school where the head is also a classroom teacher and in a situation where that classroom is near and very accessible to other staff, there has to be proof of the head's own professional ability. A slovenly classroom, poor displays, ill discipline or low standards are not acceptable in any schoolroom; they can be disastrous in the classroom of the head of a small school. Quality has not only to exist but to be apparent; it has to set the tone for the whole school. In bigger establishments, where the head does not have responsibility for a class, ability as a teacher is more likely to be assumed from the position of that person as head of a large school. That assumption is not made about heads of small schools – ability as a teacher has to be demonstrated at first hand.

Being a good class teacher does not guarantee good leadership. That comes partly from the personal qualities of the head and partly from the relationship created with staff and the actions that the head initiates. Good relationships between head and staff have to be based on trust. Whether working with one teacher or twenty, until trust is established good relationships are inhibited and the proper development of the school impeded. As schools advisers and inspectors are only too well aware, the most common mistake made by new headteachers is to try to push innovation before the staff know and trust them.

It is difficult for anyone to trust someone who is unknown to them, who is in some way hidden. Headteachers have thus to reveal something of themselves to staff. Trust and the start of a good relationship comes from knowing, respecting and hopefully liking one another. It is less likely to grow when heads make themselves remote and enigmatic. There is a school of thought in the business world which suggests that uncertainty about the reaction of a leader promotes a greater attention by those who are being led, to the tasks in hand. It is not a form of leadership which promotes trust, co-operation and teamwork and it has no place in schools.

Confidence, trust and good relationships will grow from the head proving in the first place to be totally reliable. Nothing destroys credibility faster than broken promises and heads should never make any they are not sure of honouring. It should be self-evident therefore, especially when new to a school, that heads tackle developments for which there is strong support and which are achievable. Obvious, it would seem, but a lesson many new heads appear to find hard to learn.

It was suggested that heads should let staff know something of themselves. It is equally important for heads to know their staff. In a larger primary school it is helpful if heads ensure that they have some private time each term with each member of staff. In a small school it is easier to get to know teachers as the pattern of the day's activities will bring frequent contact. A good head in a large or small school will know each member of staff as a person as well as a professional. They will know about sickness in the family, of the demanding aged parent, of new babies, of stress and joy. Schools are made up of teachers as well as children; they should be places of support as well as for giving.

With good relationships and confidence established, the head can then begin to consider more serious and far-reaching innovation. Keeping in mind that their role as innovative leader is essentially disruptive of the established order, heads have to move with caution, explaining, persuading, clarifying and enthusing. Of these perhaps the most difficult is enthusing. Promoting a feeling of success, of progress, of advance to better things is not always easy but it is nearly always possible. One of the stark contrasts in entering two schools is the feeling of optimism in one and of pessimism in the other. In one there are positive attitudes, a delight in challenge, a determination to overcome problems, the glass is half full and filling. In the other the white flag is almost visible over the door, the head hurries to the visiting adviser with yet another tale of woe and the latest restriction imposed by the authority. The glass is half empty and emptying.

It is one of the skills of a successful headteacher that he or she is able to create this bright rather than dark perspective. Normally the head is the first recipient of problems, of new restrictions, of disappointments. The head who is able to transmute these to challenges to be met and obstacles that can be overcome, who can promote positive attitudes which accept problems as part of the game and not something unfair that should not happen, is more likely to lead a successful, progressive school. The head who rushes to the staff room to break the latest bad news and uses the restrictions on LEA's economies as a shelter for inactivity deserves the frustrated and disillusioned staff this is likely to produce. However, the children certainly do not deserve such outcomes. To determinedly keep that sense of optimism and enthusiasm when restrictions are very real and when the public attitude to schools is critical rather than admiring can be very exhausting and is one of the great challenges of headship.

The need to establish trusting relationships and to enthuse staff in order that development and innovation can take place is no less real in a small school. While it is true that good relationships only have to be established with one or two colleagues, failure to do so will then automatically embrace 50% or even 100% of the staff. There is less likely to be a number of supportive teachers to help provide balance. The head's own reaction to stress and disappointment or indeed to success is often visible to staff. With visibility often goes vulnerability and heads in small schools are very visible to teachers, other staff, children and to the small community that the school serves. It is a stress factor in the headship of small schools not often recognised until experienced. Recognition of this fact is the first step in dealing with it.

The head as administrator

As an administrator the head is acting within the existing structures to try and achieve defined goals. It is not the intention to try and alter but to use these structures as the basis for reaching objectives. A good administrator will use the structures efficiently and make sure that the structures themselves are sound.

At the heart of good administration lies good communication. To succeed as an administrator, a head first has to examine the lines of communication with all staff – both teaching and non-teaching – with parents, governors, the LEA and the local community. It goes without saying that communication with the children is paramount but that falls within the role of the head as teacher rather than as administrator.

There is a tendency for the heads of small schools who see a great deal of their staff informally during the school day to feel that this negates any need for more formal meetings. It is dangerous to make this assumption. Most of the informal contact is during breaktime, over lunch or in greetings and partings before and after school. It is highly likely that children will be about and demanding attention or the crisis that punctuates most school days will arise. Teachers will be thinking about the lesson to come or the lesson just past. These are not the best occasions to sit quietly and discuss some matter of importance to the curriculum, organisation or general well-being of the school. It is important that teachers, be there two or twenty, meet together as the staff of the school, in a situation where there will be no disturbance and matters of moment to the school can be considered in calm debate. While not undervaluing informal contacts, it is still important for more formal discussion to take place and this is best done in a staff meeting.

The staff meeting, even in a very small school, should have a structure that ensures that time given to it is as efficiently used as possible. The following routines help:
  (a) Preparation and distribution by the head of an agenda well in advance of the meeting.
  (b) Circulation of any papers for discussion in good time.
  (c) The purposes of the meeting must be fully understood.
  (d) The head ensures that everyone has opportunity to express views and that younger staff members are heard.
  (e) Resolutions agreed upon are acted upon promptly.

All this is no more than good common sense but no less important for that. What is less obvious but equally important is the need for heads to resist acting in ways which are manipulative. Such methods are unfair and not productive in the long run.

Among the *don'ts* for heads at staff meetings are the following:
  (a) Do not express your own opinion too soon and too forcibly. To do so can lead to a suppression of opinion by less confident members of the staff. It can lead in some cases to a semi-automatic opposition by less supportive members even against ideas that they might have had sympathy for if arrived at by discussion.
  (b) Resist lobbying possibly sympathetic staff members before a meeting in order to ensure a suggestion of yours wins approval. In a small staff particularly, this will create divisions and the possible isolation of individuals.
  (c) Do not arrange agendas to exclude items likely to be uncomfortable for the head.
  (d) During the meeting do not contrive consensus favourable to the head and declare it when in fact it has not yet really been reached.
  (e) Do not redefine and rephrase other opinions expressed so that they appear to support that of the head.
  (f) If minutes are kept, and there should be a record of what is agreed at least, do not present them at the next meeting in ways which favour the head's own suggestions.

All these are strategies open to heads and not difficult to use if one is experienced in the chair. For the head eager for new developments they are siren voices which fair play says should be resisted.

Good communication demands more than regular staff meetings and informal contacts. Many teachers in small schools spend a short period together before or after each school day to discuss the day ahead or review the day past. This is crucial of course if the teachers are working together in a co-operative unit, but even if not, the meetings are valuable.

In many schools, large and small, heads circulate weekly a notebook with any alterations to organisation, coming events, expected visitors, etc. This may be only a reminder of something already discussed but circulated and initialled it becomes accepted information. For the head who has on the staff the fortunately rare teacher who declares, after the event or having failed to carry out a new procedure, that they were never told, this written record can avoid any misunderstanding. Heads with the pressure of a full-time teaching commitment and little secretarial help find this written reminder reassuring to themselves as well as helpful to staff.

Successful administration will also demand that the head ensures regular contacts with kitchen and cleaning staff and sets up a regular survey of the school with the caretaker. Governors are kept informed through full reports and the encouragement of regular visiting. Apart from formal contacts, governors and non-teaching staff can be drawn more fully into the life of the school. School assembly, for example, should always be open to them, perhaps to make their own special contribution. In small schools, where the variety of adult contacts through teachers alone is limited, they offer a wide range of skills and interests which their connection with the school often makes them willing to contribute to projects and other class activity. The role of the head in relation to teaching staff is developed later, in chapter 5.

It is of course very important that lines of communication to parents are kept open. On a broader front, open days, parent information evenings and the like are valuable. In day-to-day contacts the head's commitment to class teaching in a small school will make it that much more difficult to be readily available. It is important in the first instance to make it clear to all parents what the situation is and that except in emergencies the head is not available during class time. Parents need to be told therefore what times of the day or week the head will be free to answer phone calls or arrange interviews. Some headteachers also make this information clear to LEA offices, and if called to the phone while teaching remind officers of the importance of uninterrupted class time. No one bursts into a doctor's or dentist's surgery, walks into a meeting between solicitor and client or expects a university lecturer in full flow to answer the phone. Interrupting a teacher is often taken too lightly and heads of small schools are particularly vulnerable.

Good administration has to ensure that having established good systems of communication they are properly used so that not only problems and complaints are brought forward and dealt with but that suggestions and ideas for development are also aired. This means an openness on the part of the head and a confidence in others that they will be heard. It also means that having tried to solve disagreement by consensus and failed, it is accepted by everyone that the head makes a decision. Reluctance on the part of some heads to do this and the delay that follows only makes matters worse. The process of defining problems clearly, seeking a solution by consensus if possible and by the head if not, the prompt bringing to bear of resources to deal with the problem and then eventually some evaluation of the result is a well tried but very important process for heads to keep in mind.

The bread-and-butter aspects of school administration such as proper filing systems and established routines for dealing with everyday organisational matters are all important in saving precious time. It can come down often to such mundane things as adequate shelving, decent file cases and tidiness. Some small schools are starting to use inexpensive microcomputer/word processors to simplify and speed clerical chores.

The head and curriculum policy

The head is responsible for ensuring that an acceptable curriculum is evolved for the school. In doing this the head will be influenced by a number of factors. Proper regard will have to be paid to national statements on the curriculum and from the LEA. There will also be the headteacher's own educational philosophy built up from a lengthy period of experience, training, observation, reading and through discussion with other teachers and headteachers on academic councils, in-service education and training courses and curriculum development bodies. No matter how prescriptive a national curriculum may become, it is very unlikely that teachers will not also be allowed to take into consideration the special needs of their children and the special opportunities which are offered by the school's environment.

In a small school the head is not only responsible for the production of a school curriculum but will probably write it as well. A curriculum statement is not only a requirement of local and central authorities but is also a requirement of common sense. With an increasingly wide and complex curriculum it is very important that aims and objectives are stated clearly, skills and knowledge which are deemed essential or desirable are described, and personal and social qualities to be fostered are clarified. All these and some indication of the path to their achievement will be made manifest in the curriculum statement.

The process for producing a curriculum statement may have the following pattern:

    (a) An examination of present practice.
    (b) The production of a discussion paper.
    (c) A staff meeting to decide on general principles.

(d) Further meetings to fill in details.
(e) A draft document brought to staff and governors.
(f) The final statement is written.

It is less likely that in a very small school there will be a scale post holder, although in a school of over 75 pupils there may be a deputy head who can take some responsibility for producing discussion or draft documents. However, the head should draw all staff as much as possible into the production of the school's curriculum statement. There will be a great deal of experience, expertise and enthusiasm to draw upon and in many small schools teachers are willing to take on responsibility for the development of a subject area with or without a scale post. As is suggested in chapter 5, it is important both in terms of professional satisfaction and professional status that teachers are involved fully in such activity and have a proper involvement in the development of the curriculum they teach. One of the dangers of an over-centralised curriculum is the possible discouragement of new initiative and innovation by teachers – which has been a strength in British education for many years and has drawn educationists from all over the world to observe in our schools.

The growth of academic councils and curriculum development groups has enabled many headteachers from small schools to discuss curriculum policy with colleagues. Academic councils are normally based on comprehensive schools and the associated primaries. Heads meet to discuss transfer, continuity of education and co-operation between the phases but they also discuss curriculum policy. Some councils have produced common curriculum policy statements on particular subjects. This has involved the setting up of working parties of teachers from the group. A similar co-operation on curriculum takes place among the members of Co-operation of Small School groups (COSS). Such contacts can do much to overcome the limitations which isolation can bring in terms of professional discussion and access to a range of specialist knowledge. In an academic council based on a comprehensive school 'pyramid' there is of course the added bonus of links with specialist secondary-phase teachers which can be most helpful in certain subject areas.

The statement itself should not be too lengthy. It will include the aims and objectives outlined in national and LEA curriculum requirements. It will include learning skills, concepts and attitudes to be developed as well as a body of factual knowledge deemed to be essential. However, the ways in which these aims can be achieved still lie with the school and more essentially with the teacher.

The curriculum statement should be a working document. Once written they often gather dust upon a shelf. Teachers should regularly compare actual achievement with stated aim and modify educational activity accordingly. This is really very important – it is so simple to state, for example, as an aim for the school the 'development in the children of powers of observation', an important information-gathering skill. However, teachers challenged to point out activities undertaken over the past weeks specifically to develop such powers can sometimes find it difficult to identify such activities. Regular reference to the statement will help prevent this. A curriculum statement which is *to hand, to the point and to be used*, is the one which has real value. The head's duty is to see that this is the case. It will be easier to achieve if the staff have been involved as much as possible in its production.

The head and staff

This relationship is dealt with in the next chapter.

The head as evaluator

One of the problems faced by headteachers in small schools is the absence of a wide body of professional opinion among a staff of such small number. There is also a frequent isolation from external sources of advice and comparison such as other heads or educational advisers. Because of this lack of internal and external reference it becomes doubly important that the head has a clear policy for evaluating the quality of the education the school provides. National testing will provide only part of this answer as the quality of that education will depend on much more than the achievement of the broad academic standards such blanket testing reveals.

One valuable aid already suggested is the frequent reference to the curriculum objectives the school has set itself. Teachers and heads should see this as a normal part of any project or other unit of work. The head should encourage this regular process of comparing attainment with stated aims. It should be an item of discussion at staff meetings and at individual meetings between head and teacher.

It is also the headteacher's responsibility to be aware of the range of standardised tests available and in co-operation with staff use those that are most appropriate. Although there are limitations to the type of information these tests provide, used with restraint they can be helpful, more especially those that test on specific attainment. The large number of curriculum statements and suggestions issued by LEAs and central government are also helpful and can provide useful information for evaluation.

When county advisers or inspectors visit there is an opportunity to bring forward any aspect of the curriculum about which the head may be concerned. There is a not unnatural tendency to focus the visitor's attention on the school's strong points and successes. There is nothing wrong in this but it also makes good sense to invite inspection and advice on some aspect of curriculum that the head feels is less than satisfactory. Not many headteachers would be negative or foolish enough to try to disguise a suspected weakness, which most experienced advisers would soon be aware of anyway. Much better to declare the area needing improvement and seek advice and help from someone who has access to a wide range of schools and educational practice. Apart from advice such officers can sometimes offer help in acquiring resources needed to improve the quality of educational provision.

Within COSS (Co-operation of Small Schools) groups or academic councils headteachers have access to a whole range of second opinions. It is interesting – and perhaps a sign of our professional insecurity and sensitivity as teachers – that we hesitate to ask for an external second opinion on matters that give us concern, while a doctor would have no hesitation. As COSS groups and academic councils become firmly established, perhaps it will become more common for headteachers to invite a colleague to give a second opinion on some area of curriculum activity of concern to them.

From time to time the head will wish to have a major review of the standards and quality of education in the school. When this is done it is sensible to consult the county advisers and use the guidance and resources they are able to offer. Limitations on the size of LEA advisory services and the national inspectorate make the frequent review of schools impossible. Increasingly the education service has to rely on self-evaluation by schools. This can be made more effective if such internal evaluation of performance is supported by external sources of reference and help. Most advisory services are very willing to give such assistance.

In summary then, the head as evaluator of the school's performance will be helped by:

    (a) encouraging a rigorous, ongoing and ordered evaluation by all staff;
    (b) using assessment of attainment in reference to objectives as the core of this evaluation;
    (c) ensuring that the curriculum statement spells out objectives in clear terms and that these are kept constantly in mind;
    (d) making use of appropriate standardised attainment tests;
    (e) making full use of external sources of reference – advisers, inspectors, colleagues, etc.;
    (f) staging a full review of the school's performance from time to time and utilising external sources to support this;
    (g) reviewing regularly the effectiveness of the resources and equipment in use and being firm in disposing of those that are outmoded.

Headteachers will be concerned in the evaluation of teacher performance. This is discussed in chapter 5.

The head and other schools

Not too many years ago it was not unusual for the head of a small country school to have no contact with the wider world of education from one year's end to the next. An occasional visit from the county inspector and an even less frequent one from the HMI constituted the principal line of communication to the mainstream of education. There were a very limited number of courses, no Teachers' Centres and no co-operative groups or academic councils. Contacts with colleagues took place mainly at the area sports meetings or an interschool football match.

Things have changed markedly in the last 20 years and headteachers even from remote schools have the opportunity through courses, conferences, councils and COSS groups to meet colleagues far more frequently. However, visits from HMI, which is now often involved in nationwide surveys and curriculum development, are no more frequent while LEA advisory services and inspectorates are very heavily involved in in-service education and training and in curriculum development also. Contacts and co-operation with other schools offer a rich source of information, help and stimulation for headteachers working in smaller and often isolated schools. The nature of this enrichment is discussed in chapter 7. There is, however, a very important link which all heads have to establish and that is with the school to which their children go when they leave. Transfer to the secondary, middle or junior school can be quite traumatic for young children and needs to be planned carefully. Ensuring some continuity in pupils' education also calls for consultation. A checklist for headteachers in this respect may be as follows:

(a) Regular contacts between heads, receiving staff and providing staff to discuss transfer procedures and matters of curriculum continuity. Academic councils are ideally suited to provide such liaison.

(b) Transfer teaching. Teachers spend a little time working in the classrooms to which, or from which, the children transfer. For schools which have done this the first-hand knowledge gained has been well worth the trouble taken.

(c) Transfer of records and information on each child in a form agreed by both schools and provided in good time.

(d) Discussion of pupils with special needs such as gifted, handicapped or less able children.

(e) Visits by transfer children to their new school. These visits should be more than a quick walk around the school. They should provide an opportunity to grasp the geography of what is likely to be a much larger institution. Such simple matters as where the cloakrooms are, to whom they report on the first morning and where, what they do if they lose their way, and meeting their new teachers, are matters of concern to many new pupils. Some schools use videos, models and leaflets to help; many use older children as guides. A few large secondary schools have only new intake and a selected number of older pupils in the school on the first day of the autumn term. This allows staff and these pupils to see new intake well settled before the bulk of the children arrive.

(f) Included with the records transferred are samples of the children's work.

(g) There are follow-up discussions partway through the first term to pick up any problems.

(h) There should be accepted and understood methods of referral from the new to the old school during this settling-in period. Expectations can easily be pitched too high or too low for individual pupils in the receiving school.

The transfer of children, particularly from small and isolated schools where there may be very few children leaving, including perhaps only one girl or boy, should be a matter for concern and action by the head. It is one of the essential areas of contact with other schools calling for careful thought and planning. Again links with other primary schools, which include bringing pupils together, are of great value in avoiding loneliness and stress for children at the time of transfer.

The head and the community

The head's relationship with the local community is dealt with in chapter 6.

Examples of current practice

The headteacher's roles as an administrator, a leader and an evaluator have been briefly examined in this chapter and some suggestions put forward for the development of these roles. There remains, however, a small group of practical everyday problems which give headteachers great concern, cause a good deal of lost time and refuse to be solved by neat administrative theory. These problems stem from the headteacher's role in the small school as a virtual full-time class teacher and also as the school's administrator. They prompt questions very frequently when headteachers gather together. As there is little accepted wisdom to pass on it was felt a selection of answers to these questions, collected recently from a number of headteachers, may be of interest. It is meant only as an indication of the way in which a number of experienced heads try to meet these problems: it is not suggested that they are unique or even always completely successful.

Question

'How do you cope with the unexpected visitor when you are teaching?'

Answers

'I don't receive them. I ask them to leave a card or call at a later time.'

'I find parents rarely interrupt in class time. I don't see reps, and ask them to call after school.'

'I won't leave the classroom. If it is a visitor from the office they are usually willing to wait in the classroom until I am free. Often advisers get involved with the activity. Parents have been told when I am free and rarely interrupt teaching time.'

'It depends who it is. I will not see reps during class time and will only leave the classroom if it is an emergency.'

'I have put myself in a less accessible room. It is easier for a secretary or even another teacher to say that I am teaching, and suggest the visitor calls back at a certain time. If I see them it is difficult not to respond there and then to what they want.'

'I never invite parents to just "drop in". They have been told along with the office when I expect to be teaching and I expect them to acknowledge the paramount importance of teaching time. We don't expect to walk in on our doctor – we make an appointment or expect to wait until he/she is free.'

Question

'What do you do about the 'phone?'

Answers

'I have a short written response which a rota of children, who answer the phone for me use. It states that I am teaching and can only answer emergencies or very important queries. They may take a message and are able to state times when I am free. I tend to be frosty with the caller if they insist on my coming to the phone and I think it not really vital.'

'If I am in the middle of something important in the classroom I let it ring.'

'I have to answer it. I am haunted by the thought that it may be an emergency. It often is trivial. The office is very inconsiderate. It is getting worse.'

'I try to get calls filtered. If the secretary has left I use a rota of children.'

'If we let the office and parents know the times we are free of a class then they must stick to ringing at those times. Each of the office staff should have a copy of the times for ringing each school.'

Question

'With responsibilities as a full-time teacher, how do you keep in touch with what is happening in the other rooms?'

Answers

'With difficulty. I use my administrative time to visit. On Fridays I ask the teachers to each send me six of their children to show me what they are doing. It keeps me in touch with all the children in the school.'

'I try to drop in for a short chat each day at home time. I visit in my administrative time.'

'We exchange classes to use special skills. We meet for a planning session once a week after school in the teacher's room.'

'We do a lot of projects together and this means planning together and exchanging classes and groups a good deal. I spend quite a bit of time when we are doing projects together teaching in the other room. We spend two days at the Teachers' Centre during the school holidays getting our projects ready.'

'No problem, we have a shared open area with a good deal of co-operative activity.'

'We do a lot of planning together, for the year, the term and weekly – this keeps me well in touch. I have always viewed the work in the other rooms and teachers expect comment.'

'I ask for a monthly record and forecast book from the teachers. I feel this important because I can't visit often.'

Question

'Would you consider routine clerical chores that an untrained person could do the biggest drain on your professional efficiency? Do you use the computer for office purposes? Do you use parents or other volunteers to help with clerical chores?'

Answers

'Yes, although there is a limit to what can be passed over to someone outside the profession anyway, I don't use the computer or parents for office work.'

'I use the computer for storage of addresses, dates of birth, etc. I also use a label master disk. We need a classroom/clerical helper to be used as the head needs. They will need some training.'

'Yes to your first question. Yes to your second. I use the computer for the school booklet which I can update easily. I also put governors' minutes and other information on disk. I would not use volunteers in the school office because of confidentiality.'

There is a considerable disparity among LEAs in their provision of help for heads and some authorities are far more generous with provision of infant helpers, laboratory assistants, technicians, nursery assistants and the like than with clerical or classroom help for heads. While some LEAs support heads with a minimum clerical assistance of 50% plus a minimum classroom assistance of 50%, others by contrast provide just two hours daily for clerical help. Such dissipation of expensive professional time would be inconceivable in industry.

A final comment

Like many other positions of responsibility, the role of headteacher has to be experienced to be fully understood. In large school or small, final responsibility for all the multitude of activities which go on in the school is going to end at your desk. Whether it is a failing teacher, an impossible child, a dissatisfied parent or a hundred other problems, it is your job to see that the right answers are found. Keeping the boat from foundering by plugging the holes that these problems make is only half the battle; you also have to ensure that the school's performance continually improves as you steer it unerringly towards better and better times.

It is a position fraught with moments of utter panic, of disappointment, of frustration and of great satisfaction. It stems, I think, from the fact that all normal adults have an instinctive sense of responsibility towards the young. For the headteacher that responsibility is made manifest in a particularly vivid way. The school in some ways becomes an extension of the head's own psyche and anything which threatens, hurts, delights or affects the school in a hundred different ways in the end reaches home. The very number of people linked to a school as pupils, staff, parents, governors and so on, is so large that it is inevitable that something of moment is either developing, manifesting itself or just dying away.

The strain is very real and remaining sensitive and sane at the same time isn't always easy. The temptation to build up an armour of cynicism which says 'I've seen it all before – you can't hurt me', is understandable but unproductive. The solution very likely lies in an approach which accepts that the problems which arise are professional ones which are to be handled by you as a professional. If you fail at times to find the perfect answer it is the professional and not the private you that has to bear the consequence. It allows the head as a person to stay secure and thus remain sensitive to the school's needs without personal hurt. This may all seem rather obscure but hopefully heads, for whom this chapter is intended, will recognise what I am saying.

Headship of a small school is often the first headship for a teacher. Indeed there was a time when leadership of a large school was very unlikely unless 'spurs had been won' (as one county inspector was prone to say) in a small, usually rural school. But for the new head, nothing – not even if the sole other member of staff is devoted to the previous head and makes it plain, not a school caretaker who will find something to complain about in Paradise, not a school cook who can't, not a torrent of paper from the office, overwork or a cut in the General Allowance – can detract from the sheer delight of at last being in charge or dim the conviction that this school is going to be a lighthouse of educational excellence in a dark sea of ignorance. It is the best of all places to learn about school leadership and for many the happiest days of their professional life.

5 Staff support and professional development

The support of teachers in small schools, whether it is concerned with their work in the school, their professional development or their career aspirations, can pose particular problems. Headteachers, LEAs and the teachers themselves need to be aware of these difficulties and take appropriate steps to overcome them. They are often caused by the distances involved for teachers in getting to in-service centres and for support staff getting to the school. There is also the limitation on the variety of expertise and experience offered by a numerically small staff and the support the headteacher can offer when fully occupied with classroom duties.

These problems can be looked upon as challenges which can be successfully met but only if there is acceptance by the LEA that some sort of special consideration for the support of teachers in small schools may be necessary. The problems have to be analysed and confronted and solutions found through a co-operative effort by all concerned: LEAs, heads and teachers.

These challenges are considered in this chapter under the following headings:

(a) Classroom support
(b) Professional development
(c) Career aspirations
(d) Support for headteachers

(a) Classroom support

Good classroom support for teachers in small schools will start, as does so much else, with the headteacher. The first duty of the head will be to ensure that the teacher has certain basic requirements:

- Clear curriculum guidelines and targets.
- Good resources including books and audio-visual aids.
- Adequate teaching and activity space.
- Access to other facilities (hall, playing field, etc.).

Even this basic provision may not always be easy to provide. Every available inch of an old Victorian school may need to be brought into use to provide adequate teaching and activity space – with cloakrooms and corridors often featuring in a conversion to activity space. Access to a village hall or church room in a town may be the result of long negotiations with parish or church councils and the LEA. Use of a field for summer games may mean persuading a local farmer to allow occasional access while use of a park for organised games may mean approaching the city council. Journeys to a helpful neighbouring school or a district leisure centre may be needed to provide for swimming lessons and that means covering costs. Use of a kiln, duplication equipment and other expensive resources may mean action through a schools co-operative group or academic council. None is impossible but all call for initiative and perseverance on the part of the headteacher. It is, however, this type of resolute and determined action on behalf of staff and children which establishes the worth of a headteacher with those whose needs are being met.

Support from the headteacher

Direct classroom support by the headteacher is difficult because of his or her own teaching commitment. Many headteachers overcome this, to some extent, by class exchanges. Apart from the use of special skills, such exchanges do allow the headteacher to gain experience of the class, its general ambience, the children's attitudes, the quality of their work and so on. The head is then able to offer what help or guidance is thought to be necessary. It will help if the head, instead of taking some subject removed from the mainstream of the children's work, deals with some area of an activity in which they are already involved. Developing some aspect of a topic being followed by the class would be an example of this. If this course is followed it makes it easier for the headteacher to relate to the work going on and to support the teacher.

The whole process of classroom support is made easier if the headteacher and the teacher are working in the type of co-operative teaching unit described in earlier chapters of this book. Such an arrangement makes it very much simpler for the head to support the other teacher in the unit. However, the headteacher will have to guard against the possibility of other staff receiving too little attention – a third teacher perhaps working with infants in a separate room well-removed from the unit.

It has already been suggested that part of the headteacher's role as a leader will be to know the teachers as people as well as professionals and to give time to doing so. To have some understanding of personal circumstances, which may or may not affect a teacher's performance in school, is material to the head's ability to act with that understanding and sympathy towards staff which is so important to a good relationship.

It will also be important to motivate, encourage and support while always recognising and respecting that teachers have their own sense of professional responsibility, autonomy and pride. It is important for the head to draw staff into the decision-making process as fully as possible. The fostering of a sense of shared responsibility for the whole school among teachers and not just for their own class is something which can be achieved in smaller schools and indeed is a feature of many that are successful. Consultation is not difficult to arrange among two or three teachers.

Other support

There will be other sources of classroom support for the teacher which can be called upon. The most obvious of these is the helpful parent. A majority of small schools now make use of parents to provide help within classrooms. Some are used only for classroom chores such as the preparation of materials, repairs or tidying up. Many teachers go well beyond these boundaries, however, and parents help by hearing children read, cooking, helping with art and craft, swimming, with school clubs and in many other ways.

Some schools receive support from people other than parents. They seek out those in the community who have special skills or have developed interests and hobbies which are of value to children's development. When asked, many of these folk are willing to give a little time to introduce these to the children. A large number of pupils, who may otherwise have received all of their primary education from two or three adults, are thus enriched by these contacts. A few afternoons with a skilled potter, a sculptor, a weaver or a woodcarver, can prompt a lifetime interest, but more common skills and hobbies can be equally valuable.

Schools also have to be alert to the support which peripatetic LEA staff can supply. Music teachers may provide instrumental instruction, a remedial teacher coach a slow-learning pupil, or an adviser or advisory teacher give help or advice on a range of curriculum subjects. Visits will not be frequent; some small schools that work in close co-operation with others have eased that situation by gathering their budding musicians in one school for the session with the music teacher, so that sessions can be more frequent. It can be stimulating to make music with a larger number of other children and sometimes a group orchestra may emerge.

Teachers occasionally find themselves having to meet the needs of an exceptionally able or gifted pupil. Such children do have special requirements and the guidance of a specialist adviser or advisory teacher is invaluable in these circumstances in constructing suitable programmes. It is unlikely that there will be more than one or two of these children in a small school at any one time and it is important that they are able to spend some time at least with other children of similar intellect or gift. To provide this some authorities arrange for them to be brought together once or twice a month to undertake some joint activity which will give full rein to their abilities in company with their peers. Sometimes these gatherings are in a suitably sited central school or alternatively at a local comprehensive school. The children are usually taught by an advisory teacher with responsibility for such children but secondary staff may also be called upon to contribute in their special field.

Many authorities consider the provision for exceptionally able children in small schools to be as important as provision for remedial education. There are less likely to be companions equally gifted within a small school and these children are prone to hide and underuse their talents in order not to be thought too 'different'. Teachers have to be alert to the existence of these children and be able to call upon support in providing for them. The appointment of an advisory teacher for exceptionally able children should be accepted by all authorities and a proper structure of support for teachers in small schools created.

(b) Professional development

Opportunities for professional development can be inhibited for teachers in small schools by the distance from providing centres. Teachers' centres, colleges of education and university schools of education are often far enough away to make the journey after a school day very tiring, not to say expensive. Economies have restricted the growth of teacher-centre networks. One West Country authority set out to provide a teachers' centre within 20 minutes' drive of all its schools. For a while this was achieved but economies later greatly reduced that provision. Recent moves towards making each school responsible for stating its own in-service training requirements and passing the school the resources it needs to set up the necessary framework, creates obvious problems for very small schools unless they are in close touch with others and can assemble enough interested teachers to make a course viable.

It may be helpful, before looking at the practicalities of providing the means of professional development, to consider briefly what is meant by the expression 'professional development'.

The professional status of a teacher derives from training and experience, but professional vision as distinct from professional status can be restricted by the limitations of that training and experience. In trying to expand professional vision there may be a need to change the perspective through which teaching is viewed.

A starting point will be one already mentioned – to involve teachers in decision-making which concerns the whole school and is not limited to the classroom. This allows teachers to view the work within their own classroom in terms of the wider objectives of the school. This should lead on to a willingness to consider the merit in the work of other teachers and a readiness to learn from this observation. A move out of the secure womb of their own classroom, the sovereignty of their own four walls, is a sign of professional confidence: a subjective view would be that teachers are far more willing to do this now than in the past. Certainly there is much in the way of professional development to be gained by this wider area of involvement.

To extend their professional lives still further, teachers will need to look beyond the confines of the school. The simplest way to do this is of course to be familiar with the educational press and journals, to use them and to be consistent about the reading of new and established publications. A serious programme of reading is not easy to establish for a busy teacher but such reading is part of what professional development entails.

Professional development also presupposes a willingness to attend and benefit from appropriate courses and that these courses will be concerned with educational theory as well as classroom method and curriculum content. However, even this type of course attendance is not enough. A professional person should be committed to pushing forward the boundaries of understanding within the profession. As professionals, therefore, teachers should seek to take part in research, in working parties studying theory and practice, in conferences and professional associations concerned with developing a special area of education. This active participation in the development of practice and theory distinguishes the professional from the journeyman and any teacher seeking true professional development and recognition should aim to be part of this process in some way.

This is all far removed from teachers who view their professional life as limited to the classroom. From a developed view of education should come a deeper understanding of their profession and the nature of their task in the classroom and school.

For teachers in small schools seeking this type of professional expansion, special attention will need to be given to overcoming the problems caused by school size and possible isolation. This will call for help from a number of bodies but most especially from the LEA. The support of headteachers within the school has already been mentioned, and the way in which help and encouragement can be given by them, but if the teacher is to move outside the school in search of professional extension, then the efforts of the LEA in this regard are crucial. What can and should be done by the authority?

1. Ensure that the right quality and variety of course is available.
2. Accept that teachers in more remote schools have difficulty in getting to providing centres for day or evening courses and to allow for this in the timing of courses and in the travel expenses granted.
3. Exercise some positive discrimination towards teachers from remote schools when selecting membership for residential courses.
4. Make available – with the co-operation of universities and colleges – teacher fellowships and sabbatical terms for research and deal sympathetically with applications for these from teachers in remoter schools.
5. Encourage the formation of academic councils and co-operative school groups in order that more expensive and ambitious courses can be justified in remote areas and interschool teacher exchange fostered.
6. Set up infants and junior teachers' discussion groups in country districts, which meet in members' schools to discuss curriculum and other matters and initiate professional development.
7. Arrange visits from time to time to other larger schools for all teachers who work with three or fewer colleagues. These can develop into teacher exchanges for set periods, such as one afternoon a week for a term. Teachers from larger schools can bring special expertise in certain subject areas and visits can also offer an opportunity for urban teachers contemplating small school headships to experience a small school at first hand.
8. Where there are co-operative school groups or federations, the appointment by LEAs of a co-ordinator is sometimes made to facilitate co-operation between the schools. Such a person is often also responsible for the co-ordination of in-service education and training for the group. This is most helpful.
9. Set up a network of teachers' centres which bring resources and courses as close as possible to all schools.

The pressure upon teachers to update methods, change organisations, adopt new subjects or enlarge established ones, produce written curriculum statements, keep more detailed pupil records and provide information for governors and parents, etc. has reached a level of demand that would have seemed quite out of the question a few years ago. Teachers have responded to these requirements with considerable patience and many extra hours of work but with little public recognition of their efforts or understanding of the complexity of the tasks being undertaken. In a more critical public climate and with moves towards more central control of curriculum and teacher activity, confidence and professional standing have never been more important for all teachers. Moves such as those outlined above, which help a particularly exposed group of teachers to develop their professional effectiveness and understanding, become increasingly urgent.

(c) Career aspirations

Meeting the proper career aspirations of teachers in small schools is a problem that has been given a good deal of discussion time but little has been done of a practical nature to try to meet these aspirations. There is quite clearly considerable difficulty in achieving a career structure in small schools just because of their size. In a profession that has built up a hierarchical structure of promotion to meet professional aspirations and the demands of school organisation, it is impossible to create such a structure in a school with just two or three staff members, and teachers have to leave small schools to seek promotion. This is not a satisfactory situation for small schools and it says something for the attraction of teaching in small schools that the teaching force in them is as stable as it is. However, the challenge that faces those responsible for the support of small schools remains: the evolving of a career structure which will allow the reasonable aspirations of those who wish to continue in small schools to be met. We might consider this challenge at three levels – national, local authority and school.

At national level

The seven levels of promotion from Scale 1 through to Scale 4, Senior Teacher, Deputy Head and Head, which have been in existence for many years, are now being modified to give a less complicated system with three teacher levels: professional teacher, one scale for those promoted above the professional grade, and senior teacher. In addition, an allowance can be made for achievement as an outstanding classroom teacher. This should bring a new opportunity to those who teach in small schools as it could mean that an outstanding teacher in a village classroom will be able to gain this allowance without leaving the small school that he or she is serving so well.

A move towards a less extensive hierarchy does appear to offer some opportunity to teachers in small schools, opening up a line of advancement without, as in the past, changing to a larger school to gain promotion. A decision some years ago that a school with more than 75 pupils should have a deputy headteacher brought welcome promoted posts to a number of slightly larger schools. This led to some anomalous situations when numbers in primary schools fell sharply in the first half of the 1980s. Staff numbers were reduced to match pupil numbers and some schools were left with a head, a deputy head and no other teachers. 'All chiefs and no Indians!' was a less than sympathetic comment heard at the time. More seriously it does point up another difficulty in creating promoted posts in small schools.

The process of reducing staff is further complicated if the head and deputy are both junior teachers. The choice for redeployment then lies between the infants teacher or the deputy. The school has to retain its infants teacher for obvious reasons and the problem then becomes the safeguarding of the deputy head's status on being redeployed. Any system of promoted posts in smaller schools which relies on acceptance of additional responsibility has to take into consideration the possibly dramatic effect on small schools of any significant fluctuation in number and roll. It is this sort of consideration which makes the notion of promotion for classroom performance, rather than for additional responsibility, attractive for small schools although it clearly also carries with it very sensitive problems of selecting for such promotion.

At local authority level

Local authorities are restricted by central government policies and to a lesser extent by the decisions of teachers' unions when considering structures for promotion. There are, however, ways open to them which can provide promotion prospects for teachers in their small schools.

One which has been explored is the promotion of teachers within a co-operative or federated group of schools. One of the functions of such groups is to co-operate on the development of curriculum. In a large school one would expect to find a promoted teacher with special responsibility for leading development in a particular curriculum area. Within a co-operative group there can be pupil and teacher numbers equal to those in a large primary school. The promotion of a teacher within the group to take the lead in developing some aspect of the curriculum is possible and affords an opportunity for a teacher eager to take such responsibility to do so. The teacher would not be peripatetic in the sense of moving around the group to teach, although some amount of exchange teaching is usual in co-operative groups of schools. The teacher's main function, however, would be to arrange for discussion groups, to produce discussion papers, to keep abreast of new literature on the subject, to be aware of new classroom text materials and resources, to attend courses and to produce with the headteachers' approval draft curriculum statements.

Other promoted posts within co-operative groups and federations may be those for co-ordinating the co-operative activities of the group in line with policies already agreed by the headteachers. There is a need for someone other than very-hard-pressed heads to work out the details of co-operation and initiate ideas for consideration. Such posts have been created by some authorities. They can be additional to basic staffing, in which case they tend to be an appointment made to the group rather than a promoted post within one of the schools. However, if the promotion is made within the group, it offers a teacher an opportunity to remain working in small schools and still gain promotion. As the number of co-operative groups and federations grows, the opportunities for LEAs to meet the career aspirations of teachers in smaller schools in this way will increase. The making of such group appointments is a matter for great care and tact, as governors and headteachers of all the schools concerned will want some voice in the appointment. It needs clear procedures to be evolved and to be understood by all those concerned.

At school level

It does not lie within the power of the headteacher or the governors of a school to create promoted posts. They can only work within the allocation made by the LEAs who are restricted by agreed national policies. However, the headteacher in particular can play an important role in ensuring that staff gain professional fulfilment from their work, whether or not it carries with it a paid promotion. It is a subtle and sensitive process, probably more difficult to pursue successfully than the selection of teachers for promotion to paid posts. The head in a small school will probably not be able to offer the staff any promoted positions. Only a few decades ago there were very few promoted posts in primary schools other than head and – in the case of very large schools – deputy head. The great majority of primary school teachers began and ended their careers without promotion. It was sufficient to be a teacher. Those days are past and teachers looking at the rewards to be gained by promoted posts are quite reasonably and properly motivated to strive for such advancement. However, it would be quite wrong to assume that financial rewards are the only or even the main reason for teachers seeking promotion. Career satisfaction is a great deal more complex than gaining a little additional pay. It is a mixture of many things. It has to do with being given responsibility, having opportunities to break new ground, being part of decision-making processes, knowing that what is being done for the children is succeeding and that effort is recognised, and having standing as a professional. A good head can make most of these a reality for staff, whether paid promoted posts are available or not.

It is important in the first place for headteachers to be aware of the proper career aspirations of their staff. They then have to accept that these aspirations will not be met fully by the very limited number of promoted posts on offer in small schools, something which is likely to be the case regardless of the system of promotion in use. It then becomes very important for headteachers to seek ways of meeting the other elements of professional satisfaction which are not related to financial reward.

Among the actions the head can take is that of drawing teachers into the decision-making process for the school. This may mean creating a new climate, a sense of what has been termed a 'collegiate responsibility' which one finds in many other groups of professional people working together. The head must at the end of the day bear the final responsibility for the success or otherwise of the education provided in the school but there can be engendered a real participation by all the staff in the charting and implementing of the school's development. This is one action that the head can take which can bring professional standing and satisfaction to teachers. To be part of decisions which influence the aims of the school's curriculum, how the school's organisation may be improved, how resources are to be distributed, how the school's public image may be enhanced: involvement in this sort of decision moves the teacher from a purely classroom perspective to one which embraces the whole school.

Past attitudes to the place of teachers within schools are illustrated very clearly by the use of the term 'assistant teacher' which persisted for many years. No qualified doctor, dentist or architect would expect to be known as an assistant doctor, dentist or architect. The application of this term to well-qualified, often very experienced teachers, was always degrading and is indicative of the way that teachers have often been kept from the higher levels of debate about the school that they, above anyone, sustain. The picture has changed over recent years and now that there are teacher-governors and teachers serving on education committees, they are brought far more into decisions about schools and the future of education generally. The point made here is that the head must ensure that all staff, whether holders of promoted posts or not, are involved; in small schools, where there are few such posts, they must give this involvement a particular importance.

The drawing of teachers into more active roles in management, planning and decision-making means that the head will have to accept some reduction in his or her own powers. If decisions are being sought from consensus rather than being dictated, that consensus has to be genuine and not manufactured by some of the less attractive management techniques described earlier. There has to be an acceptance of some decisions which have strong backing from the staff and less enthusiasm from the head. There will be limits to this, limits imposed by the head's legal responsibility and need to defend these decisions to governors, parents and the LEA, but unless there is some willingness to compromise then staff will soon become aware that their contributions to a corporate decision are meaningless.

Other ways are also open to the head in improving professional fulfilment for the staff. The absence of a scale post does not mean that teachers are uninterested in taking responsibility for areas of curriculum development. Most – if not all – teachers have areas of special interest or expertise and wish to use them to some purpose. If the head and LEA have facilitated the sort of professional development described earlier with an imaginative and available in-service training programme, then teachers will have a much better chance of being involved in curriculum leadership. It is up to the head to see that teachers are offered opportunities for that type of leadership along with the research, involvement in development groups and course attendance that go with it, regardless of scale posts being available.

There will also be various aspects of school life other than curriculum development – from developing technological resources to liaison with playgroups – which teachers, other than the head, can take responsibility for and frequently do. Along with undertaking some administrative tasks, these extra duties can greatly enhance the quality of provision in the school, can clearly be of help to the head and can offer the teacher a fuller involvement in the life of the whole school. They can offer position, esteem and responsibility along with a sense of partnership. It goes almost without saying that negotiating this type of wider involvement calls for sensitivity on the part of headteachers; there must be no hint of exploitation or pressure. Rather, this commitment must flow from the genuine desire on the teacher's part to become involved. This desire is more likely to grow in a school where – promoted posts or not – the professional aspirations of teachers are recognised and their standing simply as teachers is given its proper dignity and worth.

(d) Support for headteachers

Any comment on support for staff must include mention of support for the headteacher. Some of the channels of support open to heads have been explored in chapter 4, but one or two other issues, relating to a proper support for the head, remain.

One issue over support very frequently mentioned at conferences of headteachers is that regarding clerical and ancillary help. To a total stranger to the school system in Britain, taking a completely objective look at its structure, the secretarial support given to headteachers would cause some puzzlement. It is hard to think of any other profession where a senior member spends so much time on non-professional tasks. This particularly applies to headteachers in small schools. One has perhaps to experience the variety and the quantity of these tasks to understand the amount of time they consume.

There is in the first place the 'interruptive' group of tasks. This includes the telephone and the unexpected caller. Few small schools have secretarial help for more than three hours daily. For the rest of the time the head is exposed to these interruptions and because of the teaching commitment almost certainly they will be interruptions during lesson time. It has been suggested earlier that headteachers should be as firm and as clear as possible about access to them during lessons, but not everyone will heed this and with no secretarial filter then interruptions for quite trivial purposes will happen far too often. Education offices could help by not telephoning small schools except during agreed hours. However, there does not seem to be any real answer to the problem of interruption except a more generous allocation of assistance.

Another serious loss of professional time is caused by the need for headteachers to carry out many routine clerical chores, for example typing and filing letters, entering dinner money, dealing with accounts and invoices and accepting deliveries. These are all tasks which in a larger school would be carried out by clerical assistants. It really is illogical that in a school where a head has to teach virtually full-time and lead the school, tasks of this sort have to be shouldered as well.

A third category is that relating to manual tasks, many of which in a larger school would be carried out by the caretaker. The caretaking and cleaning staff of a small school usually leave when the school opens and return when it closes. It would be impossible to justify the presence of a caretaker all day long in a two-room school, but as it is blocked drains, broken windows, frozen plumbing, heating failures and so on have to be dealt with by teaching staff, and the teacher concerned is most likely to be the head. Stories of qualifying as a carpenter or joining the plumbers' union have lightened many a headteachers' conference but it is actually a quite serious drain on time and energy and a distraction a busy headteacher could well do without.

Avoidable interruptions, clerical tasks which have nothing to do with a headteacher's real purpose, and manual tasks that in larger schools would be done by other people – these do cause headteachers in small schools a very serious loss of time. The role of the headteacher becomes ever more demanding as accountability increases, as longer and more detailed curriculum statements are asked for, as changes in educational methods accelerate, as resources become more complex and expensive to control, as restrictions and the deluge of returns and forms continue. The pressure on headteachers becomes ever greater and LEAs do need to consider whether headteachers in small schools can be expected to respond to the professional requirements made upon them while coping with tasks which by any standard have nothing at all to do with those requirements and in a larger school would be done by other people.

The headteacher's aide

The argument is put forward that it would be difficult to give sufficient work to a full-time school secretary in a small school. An alternative would be the appointment of a headteacher's aide. This person would double as school secretary and classroom aide for the headteacher. Such an appointment would be invaluable. It would relieve the head of clerical chores and classroom interruptions except for serious purposes or emergencies. The head could leave the room with the knowledge that at least a trusted adult who was familiar with the work of the class was present.

It would be hard to find an area of support more welcome to headteachers in small schools. It would release a fund of time and energy that could be applied to the real task of managing and leading the school. It is frequently stated that the quality of education in any school owes most to the quality of the headteacher's leadership. It makes no sense whatever to divert that teacher's time from that all-important task.

A final comment

It is a matter of some interest and purely from my own observation that our small schools appear to have more stable staffs than larger schools. I do not imply that teachers in large schools are 'unstable', of course – just that small schools appear to hold their teachers for longer periods. Why this is so isn't immediately obvious – chance of promotion other than to deputy head doesn't really exist. We hope that merit awards for outstanding classroom teaching and perhaps responsibility posts within small school co-operative groups will offer some alleviation of this situation, but these will never be thick on the ground.

What keeps teachers in small schools has a great deal to do with the bond that forms so rapidly between teachers and the children in their charge. It is a bond that gets ever tighter as one year drifts into the next and when at last that familiar group leave, the companionship of the next group is already two or three years strong. So much time is spent together; there isn't any staffroom to vanish to and if there is, no time to get there. Tea or coffee is taken in the classroom or the yard with children coming in and out of focus or swirling around you. It is hard not to join in the cricket or the rounders at lunchtime. No one else appears to take them for music or games and so you sing together and you play together.

I know of no other occupation that takes an adult so fully into the childworld as that of a teacher in a small school. Perhaps it is just that which captivates and causes so many teachers to turn their back on the promotion that they so often deserve and stay with their small schools, whether it be in a busy city street or the quiet countryside. Whatever the reason, the plain fact is that very many do stay without regret, often to become a major influence and a lifelong memory for so many children.

6 The school and the community

It has been suggested earlier that small schools often serve areas which are cohesive as communities and have strong identification with the local school. This is certainly the case in many of the villages which small schools serve but it can also be true in urban and suburban areas. In chapter 3 an illustration was given of the use of both developed and natural surroundings as the basis for social and environmental study projects and how valuable a curriculum opportunity this provided.

However, the enrichment of school life which comes from close and supportive relations with the community goes much further than the development of an area of the curriculum. Close association with the community can pervade and enrich the whole ethos of the school when that school comes to regard itself not as a discrete establishment separated from the community by its specialised function but very much a part of society, enriching and being enriched by the closeness of that alliance.

Many other countries, especially those with scattered settlements in sparsely populated countryside, tend to link their schools more closely with the local community. The Cambridge Study 'A Positivist Approach to Rural Primary Schools', published in 1981, considered rural schooling in the Scandinavian countries as an outside perspective on rural education here. The study found communities which provided and controlled a good deal of their local school's expenditure and related this expenditure to the whole development of the community in terms of transportation, housing and a wide range of facilities and amenities. There was a much more extensive use of the school as a community facility both for leisure and cultural pursuits and for further education purposes.

The Cambridge Study suggests in its recommendations that rural schools in this country would benefit from closer ties between local community and school. The setting up of 'rural community schools' with strengthened governing bodies to which LEAs would delegate some of their own administrative responsibilities is suggested. It has the attraction of opening schools to local communities and at the same time encouraging the community to play a greater part in helping to enhance the quality of education provided and thus supporting actively the case for the continuance of small schools.

However, we are here not so much concerned with *why* school and community should be in close alliance as *how* they can support and use each other to the mutual advantage and enrichment of both. What we are concerned with are the opportunities which present themselves and how these can be used. Schools which have actively sought to enter fully into the life of the community and to bring community into the school have found rich rewards indeed.

Some five years ago the Society of Education Officers and the editorial panel of *Education* set up the Schools Curriculum Award Scheme. The Award set out to identify schools which had enriched the curriculum and life of the school through its relationships and interaction with the local community. The first awards were made in 1984 at the London Institute of Education to 113 schools from all over the United Kingdom.

Schools that entered for the Award had all been visited by assessors drawn mainly from LEA advisory services and inspectorates. They discovered a rich vein of school activity which had not been investigated in such detail before. *The Schools Curriculum Award. Report 1982–1984* (Council and Education Press, 1985) highlights some of the activities relating to local communities which the assessors found going on in the schools. It illustrates graphically how much opportunity for enrichment lies just outside the school gates. Many of the activities suggested for schools in the following pages are exemplified by actual examples from the report. What is being suggested is not something that could be done but something that is actually being done successfully by dozens of schools including a large number of small primary schools, rural and urban. It is hoped that schools will take heart from this fact. This chapter ends with details of the community activity of an urban, four-teacher primary school, undeterred by cramped, ancient accommodation beside a busy road.

The community supports and uses the school

The most obvious community support for the school comes from the parents, but many other individuals can be involved in helping in the school, from grandmother to community police officer. A wide variety of societies, clubs and services from the local community may also become involved with the school, either helping it in some way or using its facilities. We look first, however, at the involvement of parents and other individuals in the school and the important part they can play in enhancing its educational provision.

Parents in school

The most common help given by parents to schools is in the raising of money to buy resources. There can be few schools now where this is not an important part of the school's finances; indeed in some schools the contribution from parent associations can outstrip the capitation allowance from the local authority. The money is usually raised by running jumble sales, 50–50 sales, fetes, winter fairs, car boot sales and the like. Parents also raise money by putting on dances and social events. Drama groups have been formed to put on concerts and plays and in a number of schools this has led to permanent amateur companies being formed, an example of how something started to help the school has also enriched the life of the community. Indeed many of the activities initiated to assist a school have important contributions to make to community life also.

Many parent groups have been very ambitious in their efforts to improve the facilities in a school. Projects as expensive as the provision of a covered swimming pool or additional classrooms are not uncommon and some of these have been achieved by quite small schools. There have of course been a few cases where the local community has undertaken the building of a new school assisted by loans from local and church education authorities, an echo of something that wealthy landowners undertook on occasion a century or more ago. Not many parent groups will aim quite so high but visitors to schools continue to be astonished by the energy and imagination shown by parents in the raising of money and the levels of finance reached.

Another area of parental help is in the servicing of resources. A good deal of a teacher's time can be spent repairing books, tools, instruments, audio-visual aids and the like. Such tasks do not often call so much for special skills as for a little time and patience. If parents do these tasks it does release teachers' professional time and is greatly appreciated by them. Some schools regularly run 'make and mend' clubs when the parent helpers gather together and make something of a social occasion out of the work. There are a number of other routine chores which parents undertake, such as the cataloguing of libraries and the sorting and tidying of resource areas and cupboards.

It is much rarer to find parents helping in the school office with some of the clerical duties – a little surprising perhaps as many have secretarial skills they would be glad to use. There may be some reluctance on the

13. Getting outside the school walls.

part of headteachers to use parents in posts which ought really to be filled by paid employees of the LEA, but one could as easily argue that classroom assistants should be employed to perform the non-professional tasks in the classroom that are now often undertaken by parents. It may be an area of assistance that in small schools especially, where lack of clerical help is one of the heaviest burdens headteachers carry, ought to be considered more often.

Thus far we have considered the help given by parents other than in direct contact with the children. Outside the classroom parents give help with children in many ways: they go with pupils and the teachers to swimming pools, on nature walks and on educational excursions, both residential and single day. Some of these residential visits can be far afield and even encompass trips abroad. It is probable that without parental help many schools would find it difficult to arrange such valuable educational experiences for the pupils. It is an equally valuable experience for the teachers and parents, with an opportunity to get to know each other and the children outside the school setting and in fresh and stimulating circumstances. Most teachers have a briefing session with parents before any major excursion is undertaken to ensure that everyone understands the purpose of the excursion and their part in it.

Matters of safety have to be discussed, proper insurance cover confirmed and parents given some idea of the ways in which they can best help the children to get full benefit from the excursion or residential visit.

Parents are involved directly with children in helping to run clubs and societies. The range of club activity is greatly increased when schools can involve parents, especially when they have special skills to offer. These skills can range from chess to archery and parents can contribute in a major way to the success of such activity. Small rural schools have some problems in arranging after-school clubs because so many of their children have to board the bus at 4 p.m. for distant farms and hamlets. However, many small urban schools run excellent clubs with parental help and some rural schools set up lunchtime clubs to overcome the 4 p.m. exodus and provide after-school clubs for those who live nearer to the school.

Parents assisting in the classroom is now accepted and common practice. It was not always so and many heads and teachers at first had serious reservations about allowing parents, who had no teacher training, to work inside the classroom. That resistance has now largely – though not entirely – disappeared. Parents now assist in a wide-ranging variety of activities. They not only help with the tasks already described which do not bring them into contact with the children but now also take part in many classroom tasks that do. They have long assisted with activities such as cooking, craft, art and needlework. Now they are frequently found working with the children, for example listening to children read, working alongside them with computers and other technical aids, using instrumental skills they may have in music, or assisting with games and taking part in drama lessons.

Some headteachers and teachers are still reluctant to use parents or other non-trained adults in direct work with children; indeed some remain dubious about their use in schools in any capacity. They express fears that some parents may use such entry into school to express unjustified criticism or may be more interested in observing their own child than being genuinely helpful. Experience has shown that such fears are largely unjustified. The parent who comes to the school for the wrong reasons tends very quickly to drop away while those who are there to offer genuine help become the school's most enthusiastic and knowledgeable supporters. Indeed, when unfair or uninformed criticism is levelled at a school it is an advantage to have members of the parent body who know the truth.

For small schools in particular the bringing of parents and other suitable adults into the school as helpers is of immense value. It not only offers aid to hard pressed headteachers and teachers but brings additional adult contact and a diversity of interests and skills to children who may otherwise be confined to the contributions of two adults, albeit trained teachers. It is a welcome development of recent years and one which all teachers in small schools should use to the full.

Adults, experts and otherwise, in school

Many other adults are willing to be general helpers in schools. Grandparents are one likely source and many schools receive help from retired people who wish to use their new-found leisure in productive ways. A number of older people who live alone have found companionship and new friendships from a weekly morning helping in school and gained much from the vitality and optimism of the children.

Apart from those who come to help in general terms in schools there are a whole range of experts who can offer more specific support. Again for the school activity seeking such support the list is very long indeed. Almost any skilled tradesman, shopkeeper, business person or professional has things of interest to tell or show the children. If the visit ties in with some project, so much the better. How much more valuable it is if children doing, for example, a project on 'People who serve us', actually talk to a nurse, a doctor, a postal worker, a refuse collector or a piano tuner rather than just look at pictures or read about such folk. Often these people are regular visitors to the school and most are willing to give a little time to talk to the children. Artists, potters, weavers and all those involved in traditional crafts have a special contribution to make and can sometimes be persuaded to talk about their crafts, to give a demonstration or even a short period of instruction. Many people follow traditional crafts as a hobby and reach high standards of achievement. They are another source of enrichment for the children. Indeed, it is always wise to be aware of local people who have taken their hobbies to high levels of skill and performance. Because of their enthusiasm they are normally very ready to visit the school and demonstrate their skills.

Talents are sometimes found in unusual settings. One North Devon junior school exploring rock pools on a lonely beach one spring day heard the sound of the bagpipes and around the headland came a lone piper. The teacher, alert to opportunities, asked the piper to play to the children. He did so and to their delight led them in true Pied Piper style along the beach. He lived in congested Glasgow and came annually to North Devon to play his pipes in solitude in the open air. Ten minutes later the same group met the Coastguard Cliff Rescue Land Rover and enjoyed yet further talk and a demonstration.

From community police officer to children's librarian there are so many people in the community ready and willing to take an interest in the school and give time to demonstrating their own particular field of expertise. Once teachers engage themselves in this relationship with people of the community who have special expertise, they find themselves opening an Aladdin's cave of rich experience for their children. The opportunity exists even in remote villages: it calls only for the teacher to be alert to this opportunity and to use it imaginatively.

Societies and associations in school

It is not only individuals from the community who offer help to the school. Associations, societies, services and identifiable groups of people also often give help. The most obvious of these is of course the Parents' Association, often broadened to include teachers and friends of the school. In smaller communities such an association can be the main expression of the community's support for the school and is quickly to the forefront when the school is threatened in any way. The school also receives help from public agencies like library and museum services. It is not uncommon now, when new schools are built in smaller towns and villages, to include a library which serves school and community. Voluntary-aided church schools will sometimes include a parish room which is used by community, school and church. This type of initiative can do much to draw the school and community into a natural and unforced partnership.

The fire and police services are often supportive of neighbourhood schools with visiting displays, films and talks. The armed forces also have very close links with schools which take the children of servicemen or serve communities close to their bases. Many schools receive very generous assistance, both financial and practical, from nearby army, navy or airforce establishments.

National organisations such as the Lion's Clubs, Rotary Clubs, the WI and so on have often been generous in their assistance to schools, as have less formalised groups like local youth clubs or senior citizen associations. There is a great fund of goodwill toward the local school in the community which will express itself in a variety of ways, at times wholly unexpected. That goodwill is just as strong, possibly stronger, in small communities where the school is visible across the village square or just beside the pavement in the main street.

There is wide and growing use of schools by organisations for meetings or social events, particularly where there is no village or community hall. In isolated situations primary schools can be used for adult or further education classes. Schools which maintain an air of welcome and where the public do not feel excluded, find themselves fully rewarded for this. However, productive relationships between school and community do not depend alone on the support of the community for the school or a welcome by the school for organisations which want to use its facilities. There has also to be a planned involvement by the school outwards into the community. We now examine some of the ways schools do get involved in the community to the mutual benefit of both.

The school supports and uses the community

Support for the community by the school takes many forms and involves a great variety of people. The most obvious recipients of support are likely to be the very young, the old, the infirm, the handicapped, and further afield the desperately deprived people of the Third World. There is also, however, a good deal of support for local organisations, annual festivals, concerts, cultural and sporting events – a wide array of activities across the whole spectrum of community life.

The very young

It is natural perhaps that primary schools should respond to the needs of the very young in the community. Contacts with the local playgroup or nursery class are common. The school may have been responsible for initiating the setting-up of the playgroup. Where a drop in pupil population has taken place the use of spare accommodation is often taken up by the playgroup. The school may lend support by offering ordering and delivery facilities from the authority's supply departments. Infants teachers may offer advice to playgroup leaders on suitable activities and resources. In some authorities a local infants school headteacher will act as a general playgroup adviser to local groups and be given some relief from teaching to perform these duties.

In one rural authority there is a mobile nursery class with a teacher travelling to villages and setting up a weekly morning or afternoon session in the local school. The close co-operation and support of schools is called for in this and some amount of spare accommodation. In remote areas the existence of a playgroup or mother-and-toddler group, often initiated by the school, has done much to break down the isolation that can be experienced by mothers living in lonely cottages or farms. Some schools have set up crèches for the children of people involved in helping in the school. Spare accommodation can be used by health care and health education staff who are then able to talk and demonstrate to groups of young parents and others, on child care and related topics. It appears a foolish economy for an authority to insist on sealing off spare accommodation which can be used so productively in these and other ways.

Increasing care is taken to inform parents of young children who are soon to start school of the procedures to be followed. Information sheets, visits and discussions are offered by staff. Links with local playgroups make the process that much easier to arrange.

The elderly

It is often claimed that there is a natural sympathy between the very young and the very old. Whether this is because both groups are outside the main decision-taking body and often less dominated by work patterns and responsibilities is speculation. Whatever the reason, it is observable that small children bring great joy to the elderly and some of the old confidence of past parenthood reasserts itself. There is a risk of tiredness, of course, which has to be monitored for both parties.

It is common practice for primary schools to have links with the old people in the local community. This leads sometimes to invitations to the school to enjoy concerts, plays, dancing, Christmas or harvest festivals and the like. Many schools have gone much further than this. They visit old people's homes to entertain them, older children look to their shopping needs if the weather is inclement, they visit and listen to stories of times past, bringing recent history to life for them. A large number of older people, still agile enough, help in local schools and, as has already been stated, gain much from the companionship and natural high spirits of the children.

There is a wealth of wisdom, experience, skill and memory among the older people of a community. For a small school the web of relationships in the smaller, closer-knit community they serve is often strong and people know each other well. Access to the special contributions of older people can be that much easier. Teachers not already doing so would be wise to investigate links with local senior citizens. It is important, not only because both the elderly and the children have much to gain, but because at a time when there are a growing number of older people we should all understand not only their needs but the great contribution they can still make to society. Schools are one very suitable channel for that contribution.

The disadvantaged

Under this heading we may include the handicapped, the infirm, the chronically sick, the socially deprived – all those who have to battle with greater obstacles than the majority of us. Schools can help these less fortunate members of society and frequently do so.

Special schools are an obvious contact. It is less likely that a village will have a special school nearby but for some small urban schools there are often opportunities to form supportive relationships. Children from the special school visit the host school to enjoy performances, concerts and plays and, on occasion, take part in some of the school's activities. Primary schools go to the special schools to view or take part in their festivals at Christmas or harvest time. Some special schools have sports days and the primary school children provide a supportive and understanding audience. Some share carol services in church or joint educational excursions. There are many opportunities to bring the children from each school together.

Special school children benefit from this involvement in the conventional school world. For the children of the primary school there are important lessons to be learned. The first is that despite their sometimes unusual appearance or behaviour, handicapped children are essentially the same as themselves. Familiarity soon brings acceptance of the differences and children can then be encouraged to offer unobtrusive help. Present policy is to bring more and more handicapped children into the mainstream of education. Acceptance and understanding by other children will be a major factor in the success or otherwise of that policy.

There is a natural sympathy among many children for those less fortunate than themselves. It can easily be lost among the bravado and primitive humour of the childworld. Early, supervised contact with the handicapped can go far to establishing compassionate attitudes. We strive as teachers to find situations where our children can learn from first-hand experience. There can be no more important quality to foster in our children than compassion for those in need of our special care, and no better way of developing it than through active participation in caring.

Helping the mentally or physically handicapped and the elderly or infirm is common in schools and can encourage the growth of caring attitudes in children but teachers are less likely to involve their young charges in direct contact with people suffering from serious illness. However, schools do express their concern by raising funds for a variety of charities concerned with research or the care of the seriously ill. Efforts of this kind are sometimes linked with the illness of one of the school's own pupils.

National charities receive very considerable help from schools. Many sponsor children in Third World countries who are in need of aid. Photographs of these children and information about them is frequently on display in the sponsoring school. This type of assistance can help to bring home the reality of deprivation by expressing it in the shape of a particular person. Famine and major disasters usually encourage a response from schools and through fetes, toy sales, sponsored swims or walks, concerts and the like, children raise very considerable sums for those in trouble.

In all this commendable activity, teachers have to be watchful that while encouraging a proper concern for others, the danger of creating anxiety or a morbid worry is avoided. Children have a right to the natural joy of childhood. All too soon they will become aware of the many problems that beset the world community. When knowledge and growing experience have prepared them to set these problems in their proper context, rationalise and understand them, this will be soon enough for the full extent of the world's sorrows to be made clear to them. It is an area calling for great sensitivity on the part of teachers. We are all aware how difficult it is for us to cope with the sadnesses of the world brought to us in such vivid form by modern communications. How much easier then for undeveloped minds and personalities to be overwhelmed by such images and for the seeds of helplessness in the face of such problems to be sown – the very opposite of the result desired. There is also a very real danger that children will come to regard the Third World as uniformly helpless and prone to disaster; to believe, for example, that every Third World child is starving. Opportunities for fostering concepts of interdependence and stewardship, qualities of sensitivity, caring and compassion are offered through the involvement of schools in their communities; they should be taken – but with care, and setting these concepts in the correct perspective.

Community activity

Schools can get involved in many kinds of community activity. Many sponsor or host Scout, Guide, Cub or Brownie troops. Others sponsor youth clubs and holiday play schemes. Small schools, especially in villages, enter fully into the traditional annual events of the community and still perform maypole or folk dances which provide the centrepiece for many a church or village fete. The occasional school has gone further than this and has re-instituted traditional events which have been allowed to lapse. One West Country school rediscovered and performed a traditional broom dance which had once been a popular feature of village life. The traditions of many villages have been given new life thanks to the efforts of teachers and pupils from the school. In urban areas, where there may be less community identity, and where the school may include children from different cultural backgrounds, events held at the school are often the only time that a considerable section of the community comes together with a common purpose.

Schools can also act directly on the local environment, both natural and developed. It may be the clearing of a stream running through a Dorset village or re-opening a forgotten sunken Devon lane; it may be waymarking on a Yorkshire moor, removing litter from a Welsh beach, making paths through a Surrey wood, clearing a disused canal or pond or helping to save wildlife threatened by urban 'development' or expansion. The variety of enterprise shown by schools in making some contribution to the improvement of the environment is wide-ranging. One school, for example, has actually developed a type of partnership with the local parish council, attended some of its meetings and planned enterprises to improve the village together. The children now have a growing pride in their village and a genuine respect for the environment in a much wider perspective. In terms of meaningful writing, reading and creative activity, these small village improvement schemes can prove most productive.

It is not only small schools in villages that contribute in this way to the environment. The Curriculum Award Report relates the story of a small school in a very congested and disadvantaged urban area, where the pupils cleared a deep ravine with a brook which ran along the back of the school. This place had been a local tip for years and was full of old mattresses, prams, bicycles and other rubbish. A member of the school's Young Ornithologists' Club suggested that the school clear up the valley. With the help of parents, staff, youth and community action groups, funds from friends, local firms and shopkeepers, and with over a thousand trees for planting, the valley is being transformed. It illustrates how a school can contribute to the improvement of the local environment and at the same time enrich the education of the children.

Contacts are sometimes made with schools which are situated in very different environments. One country school in a prosperous village not far from a large university town has close contacts with an inner London school in an area of considerable social deprivation. Both schools make residential visits; the children explore the environment together, work and play together. It would be difficult to calculate, but not hard to imagine, the effect that these new understandings will have upon the development of these children. Some schools go further afield and through town-twinning arrangements build up links with schools in France and Germany, again with great benefit to the children in enlarging understanding, breaking down barriers and bringing new and stimulating experiences.

Schools can be active then in helping to care for people. They can support and even help restore the traditions of their communities. They can generate social, educational and sporting activities by initiating or sustaining clubs, associations and movements. They can act directly upon the environment – urban or rural, natural or developed – and improve it. They can foster interest and activity in music, drama and dance. Through contacts with other schools far afield they can broaden horizons. They can make their premises and playing fields available and welcome their use by others. They can in fact not only be part of the community but get close to being the heart of it. It takes only the imagination, energy and initiative of heads and teachers who look beyond the boundary walls of their schools to the living world that lies outside and determinedly bring the two together. If anyone doubts that this can be so then 10 minutes with the Reports of the Schools Curriculum Award will dispatch those doubts.

Examples of current practice
An urban primary school

This small four-class school is situated in a central position in a busy town. It is housed in an old Victorian building of 1835. There are four classrooms and a small hall, four full-time teachers, including the head, and a part-time teacher. The school borders the pavement and playing space is restricted. It serves a small catchment area of a little over one square kilometre which is not defined by name and has no community identity other than that created by the activity of the school. The children are aged 5 to 9 years. From this unpromising position this small school has involved itself fully in the community, with resulting enrichment to both community and school.

The community in the school
People helping

As always parents lead the way in supporting the school both in and out of the classroom. One of the features of the school is the high level of parent participation in classroom activity. Helpers are not only concerned with routine repairs or maintenance of resources but in working directly with the children. This includes listening to children read, and sometimes using taped programmes to help. Assistance with cooking, needlework, woodwork and clay, art and craft, computer studies, language and auditory skills and swimming are only some of the other activities they are involved in. They also help with after-school clubs including gymnastics, guitar-playing and drama.

It is noticeable that parents are joined in some strength by other people from the community in giving this help. There are a number of grandparents and senior citizens among the helpers. Some have lost partners – the school is alert to this and offers a warm welcome, and the companionship and stimulation of young children as well as an opportunity to continue using time, energy and skills productively. Both children and helpers clearly enjoy and benefit from this association.

The school draws on help from a large number of people who have special experience or expertise. A sample list includes the following:

The community policewoman She visits the school monthly and talks to the children about relevant matters, has taken them to visit the police station and joins in some of the school's social occasions.

The children's librarian He is also a regular visitor. He reads to the children and they visit the library at intervals to master library skills, become familiar with the place and learn to delight in books. The children's art and project work is sometimes displayed in the public library.

The mother of a small baby   She is a former pupil, and has allowed groups of children to watch her tending the baby and observe its growth and development since shortly after its birth.

The Public Relations Officer of the Water Board   She made her first links with the school during a project by a class on 'Water' and since then has continued to visit from time to time.

A nursery nurse   She did part of her training at the school and still visits to talk to the children about her work.

Two school governors   They helped establish computer studies in the school and gave instruction to the children.

This is but a sample of the people involved in lending their skills or experience to the school. When projects are undertaken a number of other people from the community are drawn in on a more temporary basis. Some of these, however, continue to take an interest in the school, support its functions and offer help when it is needed.

Help from organisations

The school gets considerable support from various organisations and services. Among these are the following:

The School Association   Parents and staff are automatically members of this organisation but it also has past parents as members. The Association is involved in many matters concerning the school and is also responsible for larger-scale fund raising. Its committee, which takes the lead in most Association activities, is large – usually from 20 to 30 members. Among the major projects undertaken are the following:

– A safety wall around the swimming pool.
– A shed for the storing of PE equipment.
– The part-funding of a covered area for sand, water and creative play outside the reception infants room.
– The part-funding of a covered area to provide shelter for parents waiting for children.
– The provision of musical instruments and a music centre.
– The provision of gymnastic equipment.
– The provision of an overhead projector, slide projector, and two television sets.
– Part-funding of a microcomputer.

This gives some idea of the funding activity by the Association which of course also supports the various functions and events at the school. Money is raised through annual fetes, sales and other similar activities.

The School Association Social Committee This committee aims to give teachers, parents and their friends opportunities to socialise together. Two or three events are organised each term and include dances, barbecues, darts evenings, beetle drives, Hallowe'en parties, bonfire night parties and, more seriously, education evenings of general interest.

These events are social and informative affairs not aimed primarily at raising money. However, the Social Committee began second-hand school uniform sales many years ago as a service to parents. They were held once a month but these have developed into nearly-new sales, with any good-quality garments acceptable. Over the last two years these sales have now become popular monthly markets. To the nearly-new items have been added the wares of parents who have productive hobbies and skills. These monthly events are very sociable, well-organised affairs held in the school hall. They have become a feature of local community life and many local people unconnected with the school attend them. It presents a welcome opportunity for neighbours living in traffic-congested streets to mingle, chat, develop friendships and perhaps plan further contacts.

School Association Drama Group This group was formed in 1978. It is made up of parents, friends and parents of past pupils. It meets regularly once a week. Each term it presents one or two theatrical productions ranging from revues to plays and musicals and Saturday afternoon shows for children. At first the performances involved as many as 70 people and were staged at the High School but as costs rose more modest performances now take place in the school's own small hall. The performances usually draw capacity audiences. Senior citizens from the WRVS and Salvation Army Clubs are invited to dress rehearsals. Occasionally the group takes shows out to other venues such as the British Legion Club.

The group is self-financing and from the proceeds of shows has bought the school blackouts, stage and drama lights, records, tapes and display screens. Over the years the group has built up a considerable wardrobe from which it hires out items to other amateur drama groups.

The development of the group has been a popular and very successful initiative on the part of the School Association. It is another example of a school taking the lead in promoting an enriching activity which benefits both itself and the community. It illustrates also how the limitations of accommodation and small numbers can be overcome by determination, energy and skill.

Outside organisations The school makes use of many community services. We have seen already the use of police and library personnel. The school also has contacts with the Fire Service, which has arranged a display of artefacts in the school, the Museum Service, the Water Board, the Church and other organisations. Contact is ongoing and the drawing-in of an appropriate organisation to enrich the curriculum is an almost automatic procedure when any project is being planned.

The school in the community

The school not only draws the community into its own activity with results we have already noted but also ventures outside its walls to support and use the community.

Helping people

Once a term the older children go to the Salvation Army hall and give a concert to members of the Over-60s Club. There is tea and orange juice afterwards and a chat. The members greatly enjoy these occasions and have repaid the children by agreeing to be interviewed when the children are doing local history projects.

The children go carol singing with their parents at Christmas to raise money for local charities. The school also selects one national charity each year and the children help in raising money for this by organising events like 'The Generation Game' and sales of items they have made. Harvest Festival is a major annual event and after the service the children parcel up the food they have collected and distribute it to senior citizens in the neighbourhood.

The initiative for a street market which led to the raising of £1700 to help a training unit for the mentally handicapped came from the school. Helping people, whether inside or outside the school, is not only talked about but acted upon and the development of caring and thoughtful attitudes is fostered by this practical activity.

Joining in

The school strongly supports local events. It enters a float each year in the annual carnival. It often wins prizes but the main object is to take part, to be involved. The decoration of the float and the preparation of costumes involves children, teachers and parents in a great deal of creative activity and enjoyment.

The school also enters a display of activities in the local garden show and over a third of the children enter individual items.

The school enters the non-competitive music festival and the country dance festival. It also enters fully into the LEA's science fair.

The involvement of the school is a very important element in all these local community activities and all would be the poorer without the lively commitment of the children.

Using the environment

As might be expected in a school which involves itself so much outside the school walls, there is an excellent educational use of the local

environment. This is best illustrated by a list of recent environmental and social study projects undertaken by the school and the use made in them of visits and expert personnel.
(a) 'Water': Visit to water and sewage works. Help of Water Board School Liaison Officer.
(b) 'The Castle and Charles I': Visit to local castle, tour and talk by Schools Museum Officer.
(c) 'Incubation': The incubation of hens' and ducks' eggs.
(d) 'Farm Study': Visit to a farm.
(e) 'The Roman Villa': Talks and artefacts from the Schools Museum Officer.
(f) 'Lifeboats': Visit to lifeboat stations.
(g) 'History of Travel': Visit to Heritage Centre.
(h) 'Study of a Church': Visits, interviews with local vicar.
(i) 'Victorians': Visit to Victorian country house. Visit of lecturer from Newcastle University. Visit to Victorian Laundry Exhibition.
(j) 'Toys': Visit to Doll Museum.
(k) 'Mini-beasts': Visit to woodland area.
(l) 'Animals that Help Us': Visit of vet to school. Visit to dairy farm. Pets brought to school.

Summary

The activities of this small school illustrate well the opportunities which lie open to most schools to become involved in the local community. There is no doubt that the pupils of the school gain greatly from this close relationship with the community around them. The academic curriculum is enriched by the first-hand contacts that are established and there is no better way of learning for small children than appropriate practical activity and participation in the real thing. No study of the picture of a castle can be quite such a telling experience as standing on the battlements atop a real castle. No description of Edwardian life can be quite the same as discussion with a real live Edwardian.

We have seen also how the people of the community can become involved directly in the school, supporting the teachers in the classroom and helping the school through the enterprise of associations. We have also noted the activity of the school out in the community and the benefits that accrue to all concerned. This school would not claim to be exceptional and it is certainly not in a position which gives it special advantages. It is just that a perceptive staff and supportive parents and friends have realised the opportunities that are opened up when a school enters fully into community life and have taken those opportunities with imagination and determination. A great number of schools are equally involved and this move towards much closer relations between community and school can surely only be for the good of both.

A final comment

I have mentioned in the chapter the exciting project started in 1982 by the Society of Education Officers called the Schools Curriculum Award. The Award is aimed at acknowledging schools that use close links with the community to enhance both the quality of their curriculum and to enrich community life. As an Assessor for the Award I had an opportunity to visit a number of such schools, some of them with only three or four teachers. It was a heartening experience.

It left no doubt in my mind that a close school link with the community has much to offer both parties and that the separation of schools from their communities – a separation which is only slowly breaking down in really positive terms – has been a major weakness in our educational structure. I am not referring to campaigns for parental control of schools and their curriculum, which seems as wise as allowing patients to control the operating theatre or passengers the flight deck. As parents we may have but a fleeting interest in a particular school; the control of the curriculum surely lies more properly with professionals appointed and accountable to an elected public authority which has some continuity and represents the local community as a body.

The fuller use, by the community, of schools and the professional skills they offer and a fuller participation in the community by the school, is much more to the point. Small schools, so often lying snugly in their communities, have a wonderful opportunity to lead the way in this development. Some already do; others seem hesitant still to allow the world outside the window to flow through the school door. Judging by the Curriculum Award experience they are a shrinking minority.

The future may well see primary schools which are essentially bases from which young children go out to explore the community they are part of. Secondary schools may well become real community colleges, where older children and adults of all ages mingle to call upon the professional and other resources they need to enhance skills and enrich their lives.

7 The local education authority and the small school

Responsibilities

The 1944 Education Act placed upon each local education authority the responsibility for providing every child within its boundaries with an education appropriate to his or her age, aptitude and ability. The size of the school through which that education is normally provided does not of course affect that responsibility. Once an authority has decided to retain a small school then its duty is clear: it must ensure that the education provided by that school is appropriate to the age, aptitude and ability of each child attending it. That responsibility is inescapable.

It has been stated already that small schools possess both advantages and disadvantages compared with their larger companions. To overcome disadvantage and build on opportunity may call for special support from the LEA and the more remote the school is the more that support may have to be increased. Such support costs money and LEAs have to seek always to distribute their limited resources as wisely and fairly as possible. More expenditure on small schools may mean less on larger schools within a finite education budget. However, the underlying responsibility to ensure appropriate education within all its schools remains and has to be met.

Even if it is accepted that a small school, given proper support, can provide an effective education for pupils and the decision has been taken to retain it, the extra expenditure involved in that retention has to be justified. Among the justifications put forward is the claim by people living in remoter areas that they do not enjoy many of the facilities open to urban dwellers and that even essential services are not so readily available. Visits to doctors, dentists, health centres or a post office often mean an expensive car or bus ride. Publicly-supported theatres, museums, parks, leisure centres and libraries, for example, are not so easily reached. Although in some cases people in rural areas pay a little less in rates directly to the local authority, everyone pays full taxes to central government which in turn through rate support grants subsidises the local authority. It would seem not unreasonable for some extra expenditure on education in rural areas to be made and that is where most of our small schools are.

The cost of transporting children to other schools, the danger of overlong schooldays, the social effect of closing a village school: all these points are considered when the decision is taken to retain a school and to accept what extra expenditure is involved in sustaining it as an efficient educational institution.

Patterns of support

The support needed by small schools and given by many LEAs usually falls under three main headings: staffing, especially for curriculum needs; supplementing limited resources; and overcoming the isolation of staff and pupils and all that this implies. However, the ways in which this additional support is given to small schools can vary widely and some study of the methods used is both informative and helpful to LEAs and teachers formulating patterns of support.

Staffing

For many years small schools have been slightly more advantageously staffed than other schools. This has been seen as necessary by LEAs in order that class sizes shall be restrained where such classes are likely to contain three or four age groups. The staff-to-pupil ratio gets less generous as numbers in the school get larger. Normally when numbers reach 100, staffing ratios begin to settle in to the same pattern as for other schools in that particular authority.

As well as the small school staffing allowance, almost all authorities add an amount of extra staffing to release headteachers from their full-time class responsibilities. Headteachers in schools with fewer than 50 pupils can usually expect one half-day a week free of their classes. Although intended as an opportunity to do administrative work, most headteachers use the time allowed to look in on the other one or two classes, take small groups withdrawn from the main class or perhaps do some one-to-one remedial work. Administration continues to be a chore for the evening. Additional allowances are made in some LEAs when the school has a probationer teacher. Such allowances are a great help and many heads still teaching will recall days when the only relief from the classroom was the weekly visit of the vicar to take the junior class for half an hour after morning assembly.

As well as some assistance with basic staffing levels, peripatetic teachers have been employed by LEAs to bring additional help to small schools. In the past they were usually concerned with remedial teaching or music and often spent some of their time in larger schools. In recent years, however, there has been a change in the use of peripatetic help. Because of the emphasis placed on the value of a broadly-based curriculum and the importance of specialist leadership in establishing this, there is a greater concentration of peripatetic help in support of small schools where the range of such specialist skills is more limited. This has resulted in an interesting variety of approaches among the LEAs concerned. They are worthy of examination in some detail.

Forms of peripatetic help

(a) *County teams of advisory teachers* These teams cover a wide range of subjects including music, maths, science and remedial language. The work of these teachers is spread over schools of all sizes and is given in concentrated form over a limited period. The work is advisory as well as in the form of teaching duties. Some teams are linked to age phases (early years, etc.).

(b) *Specialist peripatetic help linked to one group of small schools* Again this help can be in specialist subjects or covering a phase such as 'early years'. Teachers may share their time each week between schools in the group or occasionally concentrate on one school for a period when a special need or development calls for it. This permanent linking of peripatetic teachers to small groups of schools is by no means a widespread practice.

(c) *Advisory teacher/co-ordinator appointed to a group of small schools* Work patterns vary but a teaching load of 75% can be demanded with the rest of the teacher's time concerned with curriculum development in the group, encouraging co-operation and arranging in-service training. The teaching pattern can vary according to need: in a school where a weakness has been noted in some curriculum area; bringing pupils from a number of schools, where their peer-group size is very limited, to work together on a project; releasing head-teachers from their classes; releasing teachers with special skills to teach at times in other schools to lift quality. The approach is flexible and responsive to need as it is seen to arise. In some LEAs this support role is provided by a seconded headteacher

who fulfils it while special funding lasts. In other LEAs this co-ordinator role that is linked to support teaching is permanent.
(d) *Release of secondary school specialists to support curriculum development in feeder schools* The release of specialists in science, environmental studies, computer studies, etc. for one half-day a week to help local primary schools to develop their programmes in these areas has been undertaken with considerable success.
(e) *Exchange of teachers between neighbouring schools* Such an exchange is intended to bring special skills into wider use and to enlarge the range of adult contacts open to the children. This is dealt with in greater detail in a later section on developing co-operation between small schools.

Resources

Perceptions of what is an adequate level of resource for a small school vary quite dramatically. Where one LEA will set out to bring provision in every school up to that provided by a newly-opened unit, another will make no special arrangements to help smaller schools.

There are a number of ways in which many authorities seek to improve the quality of resources and facilities in smaller schools. The following are some of the more common:
  (a) County-wide provision through mobile library and museum services delivering directly to schools or convenient collection points.
  (b) Area-based resource centres. These can be linked to teachers' centres, area comprehensive schools or colleges. There has been a more recent growth of resource centres related to much smaller groups of schools and dispersed throughout rural areas. In some cases these are linked to schemes where group co-ordinators have been appointed and that teacher is responsible for loan and retrieval systems. The resource centres are stocked by central grants and by contributions from the small schools for joint purchasing.
  (c) Encouraging and facilitating the sharing of more expensive resources between schools within a co-operative group. The group lists the resources and facilities available in each school which they are willing and able to share. Again, there may be joint purchasing through a common purchasing code. The sensitivity of parents and local communities, who may have made strenuous efforts to raise money for the purchase of such resources or facilities, has to be considered.

(d) Sharing facilities such as swimming pools, playing fields and halls means the movement of children and this in turn involves quite frequently the hire of transport. LEAs vary a great deal in their support in this respect. Some will not subsidise schools in this regard; others will provide a permanent minibus for use by a school group. Transport in teachers' or parents' cars is used when only small groups are concerned, generally – but not always – for special or one-off occasions. Again the sensitivity of parents and local communities, who may have played a major role in purchasing these facilities, has to be taken into account – old village rivalries can produce a crisis, a situation not unfamiliar to some headteachers.

Measures such as these have done much to alleviate the restriction in variety of resources available in a small school and access to more expensive items of equipment. It is an interesting and rather unexpected fact that where LEAs have made determined efforts to equip each school with such items as computers, recorders, videos and the like, then because of the numbers involved, children in the smaller school enjoy a more ready access to such equipment. In many country classrooms, 20 – perhaps fewer than that – junior pupils will enjoy the use of a microcomputer in their classroom while in a larger school the same machine may be shared by 200 children. The familiarity and skill of many village school children in the use of such technological aids surprises many visitors.

The role of parents and local communities in bringing the resources and facilities of their local schools in line with larger establishments must be noted. This is particularly the case where the school is long established and is, perhaps, the same school that was attended by the parents and grandparents of the present pupils. It is not unknown for the sums raised by PTAs and similar groups to exceed the LEA grant to the school for books and materials. This support is welcome, of course, but the time taken in helping to organise the events which give rise to this additional finance can take an inordinate amount of the headteacher's time, time which should be concentrated on professional challenges.

Overcoming isolation

Small schools are often country schools and as such they can be in isolated locations. While smaller schools in towns have many of the characteristics of their country cousins, isolation is not one of them; there is ample opportunity for teachers and children to enlarge their range of contacts. In the countryside this is not so easy and LEAs need to take positive steps to overcome professional isolation for the teachers and to create peer-group and other contacts for the children.

We may look briefly at the sorts of problems that geographical isolation linked to small school size can create.

For staff

(a) A lack of professional contact, support and stimulation within the school is not so easily compensated for by contacts outside.
(b) Access to centres for in-service education and training can be difficult because of distance and, for younger teachers particularly, because of a lack of public transport.
(c) Visits by county advisers and inspectors to give direct advice and support within the classroom are less frequent. Headteachers in small schools who are tied to a full-time teaching commitment themselves find it hard to compensate for this by classroom visits.

For heads

Isolation can mean lack of contact with colleagues on curriculum development and evaluation. Reviews of standards of performance by their school is more difficult where access to external reference is limited.

Clearly, LEAs have to take steps to ease the problems of isolation for all teachers. There are many ways in which this can be done – these have already been detailed in chapter 5. The isolation of children in small country schools can create problems for them – these have already been outlined in some detail. Where schools are very small these problems are intensified and children can find themselves without peer-group companions. While often this situation encourages children to make friends with older or younger children and eases relationships across the age groups, it is natural for children to need companionship from children at a similar stage of development both in and out of the classroom.

In this situation LEAs and schools themselves have taken action in a variety of ways to ease this isolation.

For pupils

(a) Encouraging schools to bring children from neighbouring schools together for music festivals, sports days, swimming galas, educational excursions, etc. LEAs need to provide support, for example by paying transport costs.
(b) Bringing children together from different schools and for different purposes within co-operative groups of schools (see pages 148–153).

(c) Linking a small school with a larger urban primary school. This has been done with great success when the country school is reasonably close to a town. Co-operation takes many forms; for instance, the children from the small school may spend one half-day a week at the large school during their last term at primary school to widen friendships before the move on to secondary education. The country school provides a rural base for excursions by the town school.

(d) The isolation of very able children or those with particular skills is a matter for concern. The setting-up of centres in one conveniently placed school (in some but not all cases the local comprehensive), is a solution favoured by some authorities. Children are regularly brought together from their country schools or any small school, for a day with their peers. Advisory teachers, some of whom are appointed as advisory teachers for gifted or very able children, work with them.

(e) Children in more remote schools can also be isolated from a sufficient variety of adult contact. This applies particularly to those from isolated farms. Schools overcome this by being alert to any opportunity which will bring an adult with interesting and appropriate skills, interests or experiences into the classroom from the local community or from within a co-operative schools group. Local potters, weavers, artists, writers, people with interesting occupations, travellers, folk back from an interesting and unusual holiday, for example, can often be persuaded to give time for a visit to the school (see chapter 6).

(f) Most small schools employ part-time teachers, usually as the headteacher's relief. Some schools have a deliberate policy of changing this teacher each year and seeking a different special skill or interest from each of those teachers employed.

Local education authority encouragement and support is vital for the initiation and sustaining of these efforts to break down the isolation of children in small rural schools. In many cases it is inexpensive and as groups are often small, transport in parents' or teachers' cars is often possible. Again, where the LEA has provided a minibus to encourage co-operation among a group of schools, the movement of children is much simplified and consequently more frequent.

In taking measures to bring greater professional contact and support for teachers in remoter small schools and in increasing peer-group and adult contact for the pupils, LEAs can contribute much to the enrichment of the curriculum and the quality of school life within these institutions.

Co-operative groups of small schools (COSS groups)

An increasing number of LEAs encourage groups of small schools within reasonable travelling distance of each other to form co-operative groups. The schools within such groups assist each other with shared resources and facilities, co-operate on educational projects and endeavour to use teachers' special skills outside their own schools. Widely known as COSS groups or federations, these groups have proved successful in helping small schools to overcome some of the problems that face them and to make best use of their special opportunities. The formation of these COSS groups has now become so common that the nature of these groups, how they are formed and how they operate is worthy of detailed examination.

COSS groups vary in size. Some are very small with only three or four neighbouring schools involved. Often these are schools which have had a long tradition of coming together for sports meetings, playing football and netball against each other, taking part in local music or dance festivals and so on, although co-operation in past years has not gone beyond these occasional and friendly contacts. More recently, however, many of these schools have come together to form permanent groupings, supporting and co-operating with each other on a much more intense and sophisticated level. Larger groupings have more often been brought together by an LEA decision and are frequently supported by permanent co-ordinator teachers and peripatetic staff attached to the group.

Whether large or small, such groups have the same overall objective: by mutual support and co-operation to ease the problems which are caused by small budgets, small staff numbers, limited facilities and isolation. COSS groups have now been in operation long enough for some comment to be made on why some succeed and flourish while others fail and break up. It is perhaps most helpful to summarise the careful steps needed to form a successful group and the type of activity which has proved to be most welcome and successful in its operation. It is necessary to distinguish between the small group of three or four neighbouring schools and the larger, area-based group of 10 or even more schools that are strongly supported by LEA resources in materials and staff. The comments and suggestions which follow relate to the former type of co-operative group in which a small number of neighbouring schools decide to work together.

Setting-up small COSS groups

An examination of the ways in which small co-operative groups have been formed in a number of LEAs suggest that there is a series of preliminary steps which need to be taken if new groups are to have firm foundations on which to build their activities. The following progression suggests itself.

Step One   Look at a local map. It is important to be realistic about distances. Distances much above five miles begin to inhibit communication and the movement of teachers and children. The closer schools are geographically, the easier co-operation will be.

Step Two   If there are neighbouring schools which could realistically form a COSS group then the initiators – whether they are county advisers or local heads – need to open a channel of communication. Heads and staff need time to get to know each other and, very importantly, each other's schools. This calls for a series of meetings which will probably take place after school and follow a preliminary meeting of the headteachers. The meetings are best held in turn in each of the schools so that there is no sense of dominance by any one school. At times one larger school, perhaps an urban primary school in a nearby town, may be involved. This can be most helpful in the growth of the group but care has to be taken to avoid any hint of 'sun and satellites' arising.

Step Three   As soon as staff know one another and the decision to form a group is taken, then it is important to establish as quickly as possible a group identity. Many groups give themselves a name that relates that group to some geographical feature – a river valley, a hill or moor, for example – some feature that relates to all the schools. This is perhaps more important than it sounds in helping to establish a collective identity.

Step Four   The listing of resources, including the special skills and interests of the teachers, is an early and practical move, the value of which can be quickly realised and thus encourage the group. This list can include the following:
– audio-visual aids and other technical apparatus (copiers, etc.)
– project kits not in constant use
– major work card sets not in constant use and similar print material
– kilns
– facilities such as swimming pools, halls, playing fields
– environmental study areas in the school grounds
– particularly rich natural environments to which the school has access: nature trails, streams, etc.
– buildings of historic or architectural interest suitable for study

- musical instruments
- any specialist subject skills that teachers may possess
- any personal interests, hobbies or skills that teachers have which have been found useful in the classroom and which they are ready to share
- names of local people who have contributed to the school with their special skills, interests or experiences and who are willing to contribute to the group

Note The group should apply to the county for a group purchasing code so that joint purchases can be added to the list.

Resources remain the property of the individual schools (unless they are jointly purchased) and should be clearly labelled with the name of the individual school.

Note – hazard warning Sharing resources between schools is not without its dangers. The author remembers the uproar caused in a village when a parent saw strange children's heads bobbing about in 'our pool' and the time it took, as the adviser, to prevent a civil war and convince local folk of what their children were gaining. It is important to inform and convince parents and the local community that sharing resources as a small school can greatly advantage their own children.

In the same way not all staff want to tell all when it comes to revealing interests and hobbies, let alone share them with other people's children. Going off to teach someone else's class in another school is not always the expected experience. A lady headteacher of 20 years' service in her own school, revered and looked up to by everyone, whose every word was hung upon by staff and pupils alike, tells of the shock of being seen as a new part-time teacher in the neighbouring school when classes were exchanged, of having to win attention, establish order and start all over again – not to mention carry her own case into school! 'Very good for me', she said.

Clearly, when resources – human or otherwise – are shared, we have to prepare parents, teachers and children, and think about and be ready for these sorts of reaction.

Step Five When headteachers and staff are quite committed to the idea of a co-operative group, their intentions should be made clear to parents and school governors. Teachers have to be very clear in their own minds about what advantages the move will offer their school before describing these to parents and governors and enlisting their support. They

The local education authority and the small school 151

	need to have discussed the whole matter thoroughly as professionals in the meetings suggested above before involving others.
Step Six	After careful planning and perhaps visits to existing COSS groups, the co-operative activity begins.

Co-operative activities within a small COSS group

The co-operation between schools within a group takes many forms and will intensify with the degree of commitment of the staff concerned. The following are examples of the types of co-operation found among these smaller COSS groups.

Teacher exchange

This involves a direct exchange of classrooms in order to bring a new teacher and new interests or some special skill to a class which may have the same teacher without interruption for four years. These exchanges may be for one day or one half-day a week. They are rarely intended to become permanent and usually last for a term or so and are then given a rest. Infant as well as junior teachers have found it refreshing to work in another classroom with other children from time to time. If there is a larger school within the group, teachers from the smaller schools have remarked on the pleasure and enrichment they have found from being involved with a bigger staff and the bustle and variety of a large school again. Teachers going out to experience the village school, some of whom may be seeking their first headship in such a school, have been similarly pleased.

Co-operative teaching

Within the group, teachers plan, implement and evaluate a project together. This will involve teachers meeting and discussing the project, which is valuable in itself for teachers who are often isolated from such teamwork and will also involve teacher exchanges so that special skills are utilised, resources are more widely used and children have a welcome contact with those from other schools. Groups sometimes mount a common exhibition of work which is displayed in all the schools in turn and can be a focus for parent attention and interest.

Teacher leadership

There is opportunity for teachers within a group of small schools to use their special skills or training to lead development of curriculum in that subject area. For headteachers who are faced by widening curriculum demands and who are not supported in their own school by specialists, and for other staff as well, such assistance can be invaluable.

This leadership is used mainly in the development of curriculum within the group as a unit or in individual schools. It is also used to advise on appropriate purchases. It is necessary for the teacher to stay abreast of the subject through reading and course attendance. Teacher exchange allows special skills to be used directly with the children from time to time. There is an opportunity for more enlightened LEAs to use such group leadership for the awarding of graded posts and overcoming one of the oft-quoted disadvantages for teachers in small schools: that there is little chance of promotion within them. Governors of schools in co-operative groups are becoming increasingly aware of the need to take into account the balance of special skills within the group when making appointments.

In-service education and training within the group

The need for LEAs to exercise a certain amount of positive discrimination in getting teachers from more isolated small schools onto residential courses and to be as generous as possible in allowing release for day courses has already been mentioned. School-based in-service training, however, remains a problem for the small school on its own with its two or three teachers. The COSS group makes such in-service training a much more practical possibility with the group working with colleges or county advisory staff to set up courses for teachers from the group. Total numbers involved can make such courses a much more viable affair, especially if they involve topics that are directly relevant to small schools and thus are more likely to involve all the teachers in the group. Regional courses sponsored by LEAs, universities and the DES for teachers from small schools have been running for many years in the West Country and over those years the majority of small schools in the area have been involved. These courses are spread through two terms of fortnightly meetings and involve two or three residential weekends. Apart from good coverage of matters important to small schools, the structure and setting up of COSS groups is a prominent feature of the course and results in many initiatives in co-operation.

It would be hard to over-emphasise the importance of these forms of in-service training for teachers whose professional isolation can be far greater than is often recognised.

Grouping pupils

Moving pupils around within the COSS group is more difficult than moving teachers. However, there are such great advantages to be gained by bringing children together for various purposes that very determined efforts should be made to do this. Children do benefit in so many ways: making music as a member of a group orchestra led by a music teacher; dancing; taking part in drama; producing concerts which involve a wide variety of children; representing the group in a football or netball team. These are all exciting possibilities for children who may spend much of their school life with perhaps fewer than half-a-dozen children of their own age. However, this cross-grouping between schools goes much further than giving the children large group experience. For example, the fourth-year junior children may be brought together once a week in one school to use the particularly good science facility in that school and be taught by someone with special skills in the subject; when projects are undertaken jointly, groups may be brought together to follow particular interests; educational visits may be shared; children from two schools may visit a third to use a nature trail or an environmental area.

The movement of children, even when the school group is small and the numbers of pupils involved not large, demands a great deal of time to organise and plan. Teachers should be wary of over-elaborate and too-ambitious schemes which can lead to exhausted staff, frustrated children and a collapse of something potentially so creative and worth while. It is probably sensible to limit these exchanges to a set period of time and then have a term or even two without too much movement. COSS groups which are well established have evolved a rhythm of intense and less intense co-operative activity which allows for planning, discussion and evaluation to take place. Much of the success of the group will depend on getting this cycle right.

Resource and facility sharing

The advantages of shared resources, of catalogues identifying their nature and location, joint purchasing arrangements, the sensitivity of parents to the sharing of resources purchased by them for their school – these and other matters concerned with this aspect of co-operation have already been dealt with on pages 148–151.

Larger co-operative groups

A number of LEAs have brought together larger numbers of small schools, usually lying in one area of the authority. Such groups often include 10 or more schools and the system works rather differently in these cases.

It is usual in these larger groups to have a permanent co-ordinator, sometimes a seconded headteacher or an advisory teacher. The pattern of work of these teachers has already been outlined. They are frequently supported by peripatetic staff. There is often a considerable commitment to resource provision by the LEA and in some cases this goes as far as the provision of a minibus for use by the group schools.

The introduction of educational support grants has allowed a number of authorities to set up these larger co-operative groups. Whether they will outlast the grant will depend on the value that the LEA perceives as arising from this input of financial resource. However, a number of these strongly supported and helpful co-operatives were in existence long before educational support grants became available and will no doubt continue.

Co-operation of the kind outlined for smaller COSS groups can take place among neighbouring schools within these larger co-operatives. They have the added advantage of permanent support from the co-ordinator and peripatetic staff and of course access to a wider selection of resources and facilities. Although the identity of the larger group remains paramount and schools relate to it and enjoy its support, it is often with two or three nearby schools that such things as teacher exchange and pupil movement takes place. It is in organising with the headteachers such co-operation and helping with its implementation that the co-ordinator has such a valuable role to play.

This pattern of a large co-operative group of schools, well resourced by the county and with permanent support staff, which allows for the co-operation within it of smaller groups of neighbouring schools, appears to have much to commend it. Certainly it is working well in a number of authorities; indeed in one LEA it has been working well since 1974. It is an increasingly popular way of supporting small schools and the availability of educational support grants which allow for pilot schemes among more authorities may increase their use still further. These grants probably offer a stronger, more secure base for co-operation than the small COSS group which operates alone, but it is important to acknowledge that many small COSS groups not enfolded within larger organisations do flourish and have done so for some years with great benefit to the schools involved.

Examples of current practice

The following are examples of the patterns of support for small schools used in three LEAs.

LEA no. 1

A project for '... the support and enrichment of the curriculum in small rural schools ...' was initiated in 1974. The LEA had a total of 75 small

schools (less than 100 on roll) at that time. A third of the schools, 25 in all, were chosen for the first phase of the project. The schools were situated in three areas. In one area there were seven schools and in the other two areas, nine each. In each of these areas the following provision was made:
(a) *An advisory teacher, scale 3*   It was his responsibility to oversee and develop the project in that area and to act as co-ordinator of the group's activities.
(b) *A peripatetic class music teacher*   She was responsible for developing music in the schools as well as organising co-operative musical activities such as festivals.
(c) *Extra teaching staff*   More staff were provided to bring staffing in line with the most favourable in any particular category.
(d) *Non-teaching staff*   The normal allocation of 15 hours per week of secretarial/ancillary help was increased to 20 hours.
(e) *Minibus*   Each area was allocated a minibus for use by the project schools free of charge. Use of the minibus was organised by the advisory teacher.
(f) *Shared equipment*   The following items were made available to each group: heat copier, jumbo typewriter, 8mm projector, 16mm projector, cine camera, spirit duplicator, kiln. These were stored at and loaned from the advisory teacher's base.
(g) *Extra equipment for each school*   All schools received equipment necessary to bring them in line with the provision of equipment made to new schools of similar size.

The LEA continued to sustain the project although the economic recession made it impossible to move to the second and third phases until 1982/83 when a further 13 schools were taken into the project. The number of small schools had increased by then to 90. In these later stages it was decided to concentrate on improving human resources as in general the level of physical resources in all schools had improved. In Phase Two the following provision was made:
(a) An advisory teacher, Scale 3.
(b) A peripatetic class music teacher.
(c) A peripatetic class teacher, early years.
(d) Five hours' extra ancillary help in each school.
(e) A minibus.
(f) A base with resources for environmental studies.

The extra staffing in each school, which had been a feature of Phase One, was not included. It had proved difficult to protect this as circumstances and numbers on roll altered and it tended to be eroded. Thus the additional peripatetic teacher appointed to each group was seen as more flexible when circumstances changed and at the same time protected the overall provision for the group.

The project, after some initial fear of lost autonomy or threat of closure, is now warmly welcomed by the schools and the LEA is moving towards provision within the project for all its smaller primary schools.

LEA no. 2

In 1980, following the Primary Survey by HMI, this LEA set up a federation or co-operative group of small schools in one of its rural areas. The declared intention was to lend support to curriculum and professional development and to increase opportunities for interschool support. Particular attention was paid to curriculum viability and the sharing of expertise among the teachers. There was also a declared intention to maximise opportunities for social and interpersonal contacts as well as professional meetings. From this came theatre visits, wine and cheese evenings, dances and other social events which helped to bring the staff from scattered rural schools together. This gave a chance for friendships and understandings to grow on which professional co-operation and trust could more easily be built.

Five more federations have been established and among these are a number of inner-city schools where the pupil roll has dropped to less than 100. A small element of over-staffing in the county's provision enabled the LEA to lend staffing support to smaller schools and by 1983 all federations had at least some additional teacher help. Each federation was also supported with a grant of £1200 to assist in the joint purchase of equipment and with the transport costs involved in co-operative activity.

In 1985 the LEA was successful in obtaining an educational support grant for small schools. This enabled appointments to be made of Scale 3 support teachers in maths, science and CDT and a general upgrading of the amount of assistance available to the federations. The grant facilitated work in a number of directions including the following:

- Support and development of the curriculum.
- Employment of support teachers to work alongside class teachers in developing good practice.
- Improvement of the provision of school-based in-service training.
- Help for federations in the development of curriculum guidelines.
- Provision of workshops to bring pupils of similar age or need in the federation schools together.
- Provision of additional resources and effective distribution and retrieval systems.

The LEA had recognised that contacts between the federations could be helpful. There is now a 'Confederation of Small Schools' at which the conveners of each federation meet regularly with members of the advisory service and the administration to consider the special needs of small schools and the effects of LEA policy on them.

The Confederation also organises county conferences, usually on a Saturday when more than 100 teachers may be involved in considering some topic relevant to small schools. This conference is considered a prestigious and important event, and the Director of Education, Chairman of the Education Committee, other invited LEA representatives and the press are in attendance.

In other parts of the country the title 'federation' has been used to denote groups of schools which have been brought together under one headteacher. However, this is not and never was the intention of this LEA; each school fully retains its autonomy and its own headteacher.

LEA no. 3

This is a mainly rural authority with a high proportion of small schools, and the special needs of this group have been recognised for many years. This has been reflected in staffing policy which has given small schools a relatively favourable pupil/teacher ratio, a standard sum of money which goes to all schools regardless of size before capitation allowance, and a programme of in-service courses directed particularly at the staffs of these schools.

Schools are organised in pyramids in rural areas, with the comprehensive secondary schools linked to their group of primary feeder schools. The liaison within these pyramids is good and has been strongly encouraged by the LEA inspectorate. The result has been a wide variety of co-operative activities involving various pairs or small groups of neighbouring schools, often drawing in the secondary school or a larger primary school within the pyramid. The activity may be aimed at some short-term objective and last for only a short period or it may be a long-standing and regular feature of the pyramid's activities.

Among the co-operative activities undertaken are the more traditional links for sports days, galas, games, music and dance festivals. The LEA has long financed bus travel to neighbouring schools to use playing fields and halls. In some cases these visits are extended to allow for joint activities in art, craft and music. Schools have joined up for educational visits, sharing the planning as well as the expense, and at times have combined with a larger school which has made a more ambitious, longer visit possible. Schools have come together to enjoy visiting speakers, travelling exhibitions and theatre companies. In one or two cases small groups of schools have combined to develop a series of nature trails for all the schools within the pyramid to use.

Added impetus was given to the co-operative movement when the LEA allowed supply cover for five days to all schools with a staff of headteacher plus six teachers (or fewer) during the school year 1984/85. This time was to be used specifically for curriculum and staff development.

Schools worked as full pyramid groups, in pairs or in interest groups of varying sizes. Many areas of the curriculum were considered and developments that were initiated then have in many cases continued.

One development of particular interest was the strong link formed between a small two-teacher primary and its secondary school. Eight of the secondary school teachers have visited this small school during their non-contact time, often taking part in the teaching.

With this considerable degree of co-operation well established – and following a DES Regional Course for Curriculum Management in Small Schools – more defined and closely linked COSS groups have begun to form within the pyramids. These groups, each of four schools, have given themselves more defined objectives which include the following:
– Sharing resources and establishing joint purchasing.
– Organising peer-group activities for their pupils.
– Supporting each other in curriculum planning and development.

The groups have developed differently as each has established its own particular needs and strengths. Some flavour of the activity taking place may be gained by the following examples of one group's activities:
– Setting up of a computer workshop.
– Pooling of knowledge of the area for environmental studies.
– Discussions on new approaches to reading.
– Increased meetings and liaison between infants teachers.
– A host school's musical expertise was also made use of during weekly visits from other schools which came primarily to do PE in the hall.
– Production and sharing of topic packs.
– Joint sports events, music festivals and folk dance workshops.
– Combining in pairs to receive a travelling theatre company.
– Regular planning meetings to look at curriculum needs and further co-operative activity.

Teachers and heads have commented on their gain from this joint professional involvement. They have stated that they feel less isolated and consider that the children in each school are being offered a broader educational experience. These pilot groups are being supported by the advisory service and a financial contribution is made by the LEA. Their development is being monitored with interest.

The development of co-operative activity from the basis of comprehensive school pyramids is an interesting example of how an essentially administrative structure can facilitate curriculum advancement and interschool support.

Summary

The extent and nature of LEA support for smaller schools is worthy of a longer and more detailed study than is possible in this short chapter. However, even a brief examination shows that support of some type over and above the normal provision is needed if these schools are to maximise the opportunities and overcome the problems which their size and often isolated location create.

It is evident that this help is forthcoming from the great majority of LEAs in that area concerned with small schools; it is also evident, even from this short study, that the nature and extent of that help varies very widely. Not all LEAs respond in the positive and imaginative way shown by the examples above, and this can only be a matter for regret. There are common features in the policies of LEAs where support for small schools is strong. It may be appropriate to conclude this chapter by stating some of them:

1 There is often a declared intention by the LEA to support and sustain its smaller schools. This has the effect of replacing fear of closure by confidence in the future and is of great importance to staff and local community.
2 The amount of help is large enough to be significant and its results are visible to teachers and others concerned. The nature of the help arises from discussion between the LEA and teachers; it is not imposed without consultation.
3 There are permanent staff, and advisory and peripatetic staff, whose time is wholly given to the support of small schools.
4 There are realistic attempts within the constraints of budgets to bring the resource provision in small schools to levels that are equal to those in larger schools.
5 The mutual help which is possible within co-operative groups is recognised. Such groups are encouraged and supported and increasingly form the medium through which LEA help is channelled. The marked growth of such groups has been a feature of small school activity over the last few years. It reflects a determination among small schools to overcome isolation and broaden the curriculum. The support of the LEA will be crucial if these objectives are to be achieved.

A final comment

As this book goes to press a new Education Act is being formulated which could very dramatically alter the relationships between local authorities and their schools. The Act will allow schools to opt out of local authority control and be run by the school governors with finance directly supplied by the central government. If schools do this in any numbers it would greatly reduce the LEA role in education and because 'He who pays the piper calls the tune', much of the control must pass to central government. Presumably schools that turn their backs on the LEA will have to look to other sources for the local support they now get from that LEA.

We have seen in the past few pages the vital role the LEA plays in creating and sustaining the small school co-operative groups which promise so much for the future. But it is not only in that role that the LEA is so important to the small school. Along with most heads I complained about 'the office' at times but from where else but the LEA would I have obtained the services I knew to be so important: school meals, school transport, school supplies, school remedial and psychological services, school library, school museum service, supply teachers, peripatetic teachers, in-service provision, county architects and surveyors – even school medical and dental services? The list could go on. That headteachers can buy in these services from as yet unstated sources is fanciful; the time needed and the cost of doing this is unimaginable and there is no alternative structure of supply. With the responsibility for employing, paying and insuring teachers also devolved by the Act on opted-out schools, heads of small schools are going to need something more than one half-day a week clear of the classroom; in fact they will be lucky to get one half-day *in* the classroom!

Finally, we have yet to be told who will monitor the standards in schools and advise on improvements. This has been done for years by LEA inspectors and advisers. Her Majesty's Inspectors have national tasks to fulfil and have not supplied this ongoing monitoring of individual schools for many years.

Whether time proves these fears groundless or not, the connection between schools and the elected body which represents the whole local community, not a narrower or more distant interest, is a proper and important one. I should view its diminution with sorrow.

Postscript

Within the confines of this short book it has been possible only to consider some of the more obvious areas of advantage and disadvantage that go with teaching in a small school and to make suggestions regarding them. The intention has been to cover ground that all teachers in small schools will recognise as common to their experience and to make suggestions that they may find helpful in their work. However, there is diversity among small schools and there are challenges and opportunities which will not be common to all. It has not been possible to deal with many of these without extending this publication beyond its intended range.

There is, for instance, the challenge met in many schools, both large and small, relating to mixed languages within the class. Teaching a multi-lingual class has been the subject of special study and wide debate. Its problems and solutions are not unique to small schools but apply to all schools dealing with such groupings. However, for teachers of such classes in small schools, already dealing with wide age and ability ranges, is added this particular dimension of language. While this poses additional problems it can be claimed that the secure environment and the ease of communication which the small school so often offers can be important factors in helping teachers to meet these challenges. The support of peripatetic help may be needed but the nature of small schools orientates away from rejection and towards acceptance which is the first and vital step in successful communication. The small school can also offer an individual status and importance which comes from having a special contribution to make to the collective variety of experience.

Again there is an obvious difference in the situation which faces the small inner-city school and the small rural school. The latter may enjoy access to a rich natural environment but suffer more severely from isolation, while the former has less access to the countryside but enjoys easier access to the support of museums, libraries, resource banks and the like. The balance of advantage and disadvantage will alter from school to school according to location and background. For some there are special problems connected with severe social deprivation; for others the problems stem from the high expectations of the privileged. However, our concern has been with challenges and opportunities which are common to all small schools and these are numerous enough.

It has been suggested earlier that one of the prime purposes of education must be to give people the ability to think for themselves, to be able to assemble and verify information in order to make rational, balanced, sensitive choices and decisions which will be of benefit to themselves or others. The life-journey of all people brings us continually to crossroads of decision and choice – some important, some less so. The chances of our making the right decisions which lead to fulfilled and useful lives will depend largely on the quality of the education and experiences we have encountered. It is the influence of the teacher in this process that makes their role such an important one.

The balance between the individual's instinct to do what is satisfying for his or her own needs and the demands of a society concerned with the needs of the community and ultimately its survival, has to be held. It offers teachers their greatest challenge. On the one hand they are pledged to defend the unique qualities and individuality of each child but at the same time they are the employed conveyors of society's values and knowledge. To overindulge personal freedom and the satisfying of instinct must lead eventually to the jungle; to subordinate all activity to the dictates of society is to endanger that society with atrophy from lack of challenge, development and change in established social patterns.

If this balance is to be successfully held, the need for the individual to make personal choices with some regard to the well-being of society becomes very important. Schools have to assist, and in some instances lead, in the process of giving to each child the skill to make choices based on validated information with all that means in information-gathering and other skills. But it is equally the school's task to make its pupils aware of their responsibilities to others and sensitive to the needs of the community they live in. Small schools are well placed to meet this challenge with their emphasis on self-directed activity and shared responsibility. The opportunity for involvement in the life of the community also offers an early understanding of the nature of society and the interdependence of its members.

What of the future for small schools? Mariansleigh and Romansleigh Parochial still stands but there are no children's voices in the classrooms or laughter in the playground. It has been shut for many years and because it stands halfway between the two settlements it has not been taken into use as a hall. It has shared the fate of many hundreds of small schools all over the country reflecting different population patterns and a sharp drop in the number of farm workers since the War. However, there are still hundreds of small schools in the countryside and a fall in the primary school population has caused reductions in the size of many town schools. The small school is very much alive and prospering, and there are signs of a greater appreciation of the unique qualities it possesses and a greater willingness to defend it.

There are, however, new influences abroad in education. There is a greatly enhanced parental interest and influence on the nature of the curriculum and this is a process encouraged by central government. There is a greater accountability to governors and to local authorities. From all quarters seems to come an unending demand for greater breadth to the curriculum and for an apparently endless rise in academic standards even if the potential of children remains the same and adequate resources are denied. In many ways small schools are well placed to meet these new challenges. We have seen how small schools can be closely involved with the community and benefit from these links. We have seen how co-operation with neighbouring schools can offset any lack of facilities or resources and enlarge the range of teacher expertise while still allowing schools to remain autonomous and situated within their natural communities.

It isn't possible to foresee the pattern that schooling will take in the more distant future. It is only in relatively recent years that in order to teach children how to live fulfilled lives in society we have separated them for most of the day by high school walls from the very community we wish them to learn about. We can and do create childhood ghettos that alienate rather than provide further integration. The natural and traditional learning place for the small child has always been within its family and its immediate community, where it feels known and secure. The small school can offer something not too far removed from that, and from this fact, I believe, stems its basic strength and attraction. We see a move in the secondary field to open up schools to the public with adults coming to share tuition for examinations and to share facilities such as libraries and sports halls, while some provide creche and restaurant facilities. It comes as no surprise that the gulf which often exists between adult and teenager is lessened when the ritual separation is avoided and the school allows for continued assimilation.

We appear to be at a Y-junction in education now. In one direction lies a road which leads to a centrally prescribed curriculum with children forced to conform to it by frequent testing and a strong element of competition between schools. The other road follows a belief that we tailor education to the needs of the child, that each child is unique and that true education is about preserving that uniqueness while enabling that person to live happily and productively within society. Small schools, it seems to me, are particularly well placed to follow the second road. Heaven help us all if we follow the first.

Further Reading

Bell, A. and Figworth, A. *The Small Rural Primary School: a matter of quality* (Falmer Press, 1987)

Cambridge Institute of Education *A Positive Approach to Rural Primary Schools* (University of Cambridge Department of Education, 1981)

Comber, L.C. *Education in Rural Areas and the problems of School Closure* (Department of Educational Enquiry, University of Aston, 1977)

Davies, E. *The Small Primary School: problem or paradigm* (Forum 17, Summer 1975)

Department of Environment and Department of Education and Science *The Social Effects of Rural Primary School Reorganisation in England* (University of Aston in Birmingham, 1981)

Edmunds, E. and Bessai, F. *The Myth and Reality of Small Schools* (Head Teachers Review, 1977)

Halpin, A. *Theory and Research in Administration* (Macmillan, 1966)

Hoyle, E. 'Leadership and decision-making' in Hughes, M. (Ed) *Administering Education: International Challenge* (Athlone Press, 1976)

Lipham, J. M. 'Leadership and administration' in Griffiths, D. E. (Ed) *Behavioural Science and Educational Administration* (University of Chicago Press, 1964)

Nash, R. *Perceptions of the Village School* (University College of Wales, 1976)

Nash, R. *Schooling in Rural Societies* (Methuen, 1980)

Primary Education in England: A survey by H M Inspectors of Schools (HMSO, 1970)

Primary Education in Rural Wales, Welsh Office Education Survey No 6 (HMSO, 1978)

Smith, R.T. *A rural school* (Macmillan Education, 1971).